UNIV

Martin
Tel

A

TITI

Acc

THE JUVENILE LIBRARY

General Editor: Brian W. Alderson

M. NANCY CUTT

Mrs. Sherwood
and her Books for Children

'But children's books were scarce in those days; one can almost count them upon one's fingers. There was Mrs. Sherwood's *Fairchild Family*, her *Infant's Progress*, her *Henry and His Bearer*, her *Woodman and His Dog Caesar*. How the modern child would sneer at Mrs. Sherwood and her goody-goody tales! One sometimes wonders what the grown-up people of that generation would have thought of filling little heads with sensational stories of ragged London depravity, like those which do duty for Sunday books nowadays. But each age to its own liking. Mrs. Sherwood's homely inventions came quite naturally, and were very palatable food to the children of fifty years ago, and the remembrance of them is even beautiful in their eyes.'

From the *Memoir of Annie Keary* By Her Sister. London, 1882

Portrait of Mrs. Sherwood.

Mrs. Sherwood

and her Books for Children

A STUDY BY

M. NANCY CUTT

WITH FACSIMILE REPRODUCTIONS OF

The Little Woodman and his Dog Caesar

AND

Soffrona and her Cat Muff

LONDON

OXFORD UNIVERSITY PRESS

1974

Oxford University Press, Ely House, London W.1.

GLASGOW NEW YORK TORONTO MELBOURNE WELLINGTON
CAPE TOWN IBADAN NAIROBI DAR ES SALAAM LUSAKA ADDIS ABABA
DELHI BOMBAY CALCUTTA MADRAS KARACHI LAHORE DACCA
KUALA LUMPUR SINGAPORE HONG KONG TOKYO

ISBN 0 19 278010 7

© M. Nancy Cutt 1974

First published in this edition 1974

Printed in Great Britain by
Fletcher & Son Ltd, Norwich

EDITORIAL NOTE AND ACKNOWLEDGEMENTS

It has not been easy to fit Mrs. Sherwood into the pattern established for volumes in The Juvenile Library. Her works are so many and various, and they open up so many subjects for discussion, that a treatment of them on the modest scale of the present series must necessarily involve compromise.

For reasons that are largely self-explanatory, the section of the book best lending itself to modification has proved to be the Bibliography, where a number of details have been drastically curtailed in the interests of providing as complete a list as possible of Mrs. Sherwood's publications. The methods adopted in compiling the list are explained in an Introduction on page 115, but it should be mentioned here that the serial numbering of Mrs. Sherwood's books has been adopted in the text of Mrs. Cutt's Study on occasions when it could help to save space. The Bibliography has also been indexed, in order to help further with cross-references from text to list.

Some surprise may also be evoked by the decision to reproduce in facsimile two of Mrs. Sherwood's lesser-known works, rather than, say, *The History of the Fairchild Family*, or a full-length story such as *Shanty the Blacksmith*. The two chosen examples of her writing, however, do enable us to show, on however small a scale, something of Mrs. Sherwood's attitude to her craft during the eighteen-twenties—a point enlarged upon by Mrs. Cutt in her discussion of the facsimiles in Chapter Six.

In acknowledging help received on this book, the Series Editor and Mrs. Cutt would like first of all to record their gratitude to Sister April O'Leary of the Digby Stuart College of Education, Roehampton, for her invaluable assistance with bibliographical details and locations; to Miss Judith St. John and her staff at the Osborne Collection, Toronto Public Library; to Miss Alison Maude and Mr. Patterson of the Interlibrary Loan Office of the University of Victoria; Mr. Heaney of the Philadelphia Free Library for arranging loan of catalogues of the American Tract Society; Mr. Schalow of the Presbyterian Historical Society, Philadelphia; Mr. Thomas of the Shrewsbury Library; R. A. Brimmell of Hastings; H. Kessler of Poor Richard's Bookshop, Victoria, B.C.; R. D. Hilton Smith of the Adelphi Bookshop, Victoria, B.C.; also Miss Whalley, Miss Weedon, Mrs. Renier and Mrs. Mary Ørvig who have answered questions or checked details.

The following libraries and collections visited in the course of research have made the effort a pleasure rather than a task:

Birmingham Reference Library and the Parker Collection; Bodleian Library and John Johnson Collection, Oxford; British Museum Reading Room and Newspaper Library, Colindale; Evangelical Library, London; London Library; Scottish National Library, Edinburgh; Shrewsbury Library; Toronto Public Library, the Osborne Collection; University of British Columbia Library and Rare Book Room; University of London Library; University of Victoria Library and Rare Book Room; Victoria and Albert Museum Library.

The following libraries and collections have generously made available lists and details of their holdings of Mrs. Sherwood's books:

American Antiquarian Society, Worcester, Mass.; Boston Public Library; Columbia University, Teachers' College Library; Butler Library; Henry Huntington Museum Library; Newberry Library, Chicago; New York Public Library and Donnell Library Centre, N.Y.; Philadelphia Free Library; University of Harvard; University of Michigan, Ann Arbor; University of Nottingham; Utica Public Library; Yale University.

The author acknowledges with gratitude the Canada Research Grant which made it possible to work in London; and a travel Grant from the University of Victoria.

M.N.C.
B.W.A.

CONTENTS

PREFACE

No study of nineteenth-century children's books in England can afford to ignore Mrs. Sherwood. In sheer bulk alone the body of her writings towers over that of any other children's writer of the times: over four hundred different titles—books, tales, tracts, texts, magazines, articles in periodicals, chapbooks, and Sunday School rewards—can be identified. The check-list on which Sister April O'Leary is working (which has helped to form the Bibliography of the present book) already numbers some 420 titles; there may be more.

The following survey attempts to show Mrs. Sherwood in the context of her own times rather than from the vantage point of a permissive, post-Freudian twentieth century; and to account to some extent for her remarkable influence upon Victorian literature for the young. During the fifty years in which she was writing, Mrs. Sherwood furnished both the bookshelves of the nursery and the minds of its occupants. To determine after a hundred and fifty years how far she may be held responsible for perpetuating Evangelical attitudes and assumptions is difficult; but certainly the first generation of her readers grew up to shape the Victorian world. As members of the ruling class at home and in the colonies, they became officers of army, navy, and merchant marine; clergymen and missionaries; businessmen and writers. Kingsley asserting that the domestic relations exist to teach the divine could have had that theory impressed on him in his Evangelical childhood; Bishop Samuel Wilberforce, although no Evangelical by the time he wrote *Agathos and Other Stories*, did it in the allegorical fashion made popular by Mrs. Sherwood. Macaulay's *History of England* is an expression of the Evangelical view of irreconcilable good and evil operating in the world. Marian Evans and Charlotte and Emily Brontë were daughters of Evangelical homes.

Theories diffused by Mrs. Sherwood's writings dominated education for half a century; and governed missionary activity abroad. Although Mrs. Sherwood did not originate these theories—in fact, as will be shown, she originated very little —her presentation of Evangelical doctrine was understandable, even attractive, to children, and her picture of India detailed and dramatic. The effect of her writings in shaping the assumptions behind the Victorian missionary movement is probably greater than has been realized, while in America, her popularity, though of shorter duration than in England, helped to form children's taste for narrative literature before the appearance of home-grown Sunday School writers.

For the purposes of the present survey, Mrs. Sherwood's literary career has been seen as though divided into three periods:

1. 1795–1805: works which were not written for children. Two novels of high life, *The Traditions* and *Margarita*, published with the Minerva Press before 1800, belong to the eighteenth-century school of sentimental romance; the two tract novels of village life, *The History of Susan Gray* and *The History of Lucy Clare*, look forward to their writer's Evangelical period. Before 1805, she had shown herself to be not only a romantic and senti-mental writer, but also one of strong moral and religious ten-dencies which came under the approval of Mrs. Trimmer herself:

... in the form of a most interesting and affecting narrative, all the arguments which Reason and Religion can furnish ... enforced by the most striking examples of *persevering Virtue,* triumphing even over death and the grave ... (Review of *The History of Susan Gray* in *The Guardian of Education,* Vol I, 1802, p. 267.)

2. 1810–(?1830): the writings of Mrs. Sherwood's Evangelical period. Covering the years of her residence in India and extend-ing to about 1826, this period strongly influenced the history of Victorian children's books. The Indian stories, varied in style, extended the range of the religious tract; they were followed by a mass of educational and didactic material, to some extent varied to meet the 'house-style' of a group of influential religious publishers. Through the vigour of these houses her works for children were made available to the young of all classes in a society where literacy was advancing and Sunday Reading becoming a fixed habit.

3. (?1830)–1851: Mrs. Sherwood's post-Evangelical period. A study of her books after 1826 indicates that the generally accepted picture of Mrs. Sherwood as *only* an Evangelical writer is mis-leading. As author of *The History of the Fairchild Family*, Part I, she is herself partly to blame for this misconception; but critics who have neglected the rest of her writing, and the order in which her books appeared, are also at fault. Unfavourable comparisons drawn between *The History of The Fairchild Family* of 1818 and Catherine Sinclair's *Holiday House* (1839), for instance, prefer to ignore the existence of Part II of *The History of The Fairchild Family* (1842), a book which demonstrates clearly that

around 1840 Mrs. Sherwood and Catherine Sinclair had many ideas in common (including the value of death-bed scenes).

Too little is known about Mrs. Sherwood as a precursor of the Victorian domestic tale for children. The Evangelicals who had been delighted to enrol her in their ranks in 1814 were equally delighted to get rid of her fifteen years later. Having helped to establish the strong Evangelical grip on children's books, Mrs. Sherwood, before 1830, lapsed, took up Millenarianism and became an unashamed novelist whose subsequent writing opened the flood-gates of juvenile fiction.

The facsimiles have been selected to give as far as possible a balanced view of Mrs. Sherwood's writing for the very young during the years in which she rose to fame. *The Little Woodman and his Dog Caesar*, of the same period as *The History of the Fairchild Family*, Part I, displays similar religious teaching, but in a simpler form. The chapbook, *Soffrona and her Cat Muff*, published in the 1820's, like so many of Mrs. Sherwood's shorter tales, indicates in its lively detail and sympathetic presentation of childish emotion that she was just as much a precursor of Mrs. Ewing and Mrs. Molesworth as she was the literary descendant of Bunyan and Janeway.

A Sketch of Mrs. Sherwood's Life

Mrs. Sherwood was born in 1775, eldest daughter and second child of the Reverend George Butt, Rector of Stanford, near Worcester. Her father, at one period Chaplain to George III, was an excellent type of eighteenth-century clergyman, charitable, tolerant, scholarly, a genuine if not fervent Christian. Later generations which looked askance at his plurality of benefices would have been unable to match his cordial relationship with dissenting neighbours or his enlightened view of education. His children enjoyed a thoroughly happy childhood. Mary Butt knew a degree of personal freedom which was to be quite unthought of for children of her social class in Victorian times; although for several hours a day she wore an iron collar and a back-board to correct her slouch, she also had the run of the near-by woods and fields, was educated with her brother in Latin and Greek, and browsed in her father's extensive library. When she represents in her books a happy family life as the earthly type of heavenly order, she testifies to her own memories of childhood.

From sixteen to eighteen, she attended the Abbey School at Reading, an approved private school for daughters of the clergy and minor gentry, which counted among earlier pupils Cassandra and Jane Austen. She enjoyed her two years at school, and left with a considerable degree of social polish and a good knowledge of elegant conversational French.

For the next two years she went out a good deal in county society, where her looks attracted favourable attention. A graceful dancer, unusually tall, with beautiful curly auburn hair, she must have been an extremely handsome girl. This period of her life was short: from the age of twenty-one, she was swept into the stream of rapidly changing religious thought and belief. The excesses of the Revolution in France, the miseries attendant upon the endless war, the unexpected death of her father in 1796, and the separation from her cousin, Henry Sherwood, to whom she had a strong attachment, all worked upon a temperament naturally serious, intense, and devout. Mrs. Butt, timid and withdrawn, insisted upon retiring after her husband's death to an uncomfortable house in Bridgnorth, where she became a near-recluse. Under these circumstances, it was natural that her daughters should brood upon the vicissitudes of life from which their youthful happiness and gaiety had been swiftly swept away.

Mary Butt and her younger sister Lucy turned to Sunday School work on the lines laid down by Hannah More. Mary found it satisfying and developed her natural gift for teaching. Both sisters wrote stories based on their experiences at this time: Lucy, *The History of Margaret Whyte*, and Mary, *The History of Susan Gray*, a sort of purified *Pamela* for the instruction of her large class of young village women and girls.

In 1803 Mary Butt married her cousin, Henry Sherwood, who had returned safely from military service in the West Indies. She was then twenty-eight, he, twenty-six. For over two years she followed the 53rd Regiment around England, amassing a first-hand knowledge of army life and of its effects upon the lives of soldiers' wives and children which she later used in a number of tracts and stories (e.g. C3; C4; D6).

Her first child, Mary Henrietta, was born in 1804 and ten months later, the 53rd Regiment was ordered to India. Leaving the infant with her mother and sister, Mrs. Sherwood embarked in April 1805 for the journey that ushered in the most painful and significant decade of her long life.

During a wretchedly uncomfortable and, at times, dangerous five-month voyage in an overcrowded East Indiaman, her well-developed Evangelical urge crystallized out into action. Refusing to accept the journey as a period of enforced idleness, she kept a detailed journal, picturing vividly her makeshift cabin through which passed the muzzle of a great gun, and where the foul water from the scuppers washed across the floor; the great storm with waterspouts rising from the sea on all sides; the near-capture by French warships. She methodically studied the Bible with her husband; assumed almost full care of the baby belonging to a soldier's wife who waited upon her; taught a soldier's little boy to read. Through much of the voyage she was suffering the sickness of early pregnancy, but there is no word of complaint.

As a letter to her family in October 1805 indicates, she had, even then, decided that her appointed work lay in the religious education of the young and of the heathen.

Just after her arrival, on a visit to the home of 'one of the first persons in Calcutta', she had been welcomed by a child:

... a little delicate boy about four years of age came very prettily to meet me & took hold of my hand & led me up the stairs. The only English words he could speak were how do you do but he could talk the Native language very fluently. Is it not dreadful to leave children to such an age as this to the entire management not only of servants but of Pagans, & the horrid profligacy of Pagans may be conjectured by what I am told is visible in their worship & religious ceremonies. . . . The Europeans here know this, they often speak of it, yet they leave their children entirely to them. . . .

Please God I should ever be tried I will take warning from the experience of others and never will trust a Christian lamb within the jaws of the Lion who goes about seeking whom he may devour. I do not blame the poor natives of the country . . . the time I hope will come when the glorious light of Christianity will shine upon them . . .*

Here, obviously, is the genesis of one of her most famous books, *The History of Little Henry and his Bearer*. *Little Henry* was named for the child she bore in 1805 and lost less than two years later; but in all other respects he is the child who greeted her in Calcutta and became for her and for her readers the prototype of the missionary child.

The next ten years of Mrs. Sherwood's life was a period of unremitting activity of a sort unheard of for a woman of her station in her particular circumstances. She lived under enormous strain, augmented by an inner turmoil of emotion: religious conviction that she could not clarify for many years; grief over the illness and death of two

* Mrs. Sherwood to her family in England. From the *Cameron Commonplace Book*, now in the possession of the Osborne Collection of Early Children's Books, Toronto Public Library. The book belonged to Charles Cameron, Mrs. Sherwood's nephew.

children; concern over the situation of the children of the barracks. Heightened feeling gave to her writing of those years the intensity that sets it above most of the work of the more tranquil days to follow.

On their return from India in 1816, the Sherwoods settled near Worcester. Since Captain Sherwood's future with the army was uncertain and they had five children and two adopted orphans to bring up, his wife prepared to open a small, select boarding-school for girls. She conducted it successfully from 1818 to 1830 along lines that she describes in her own school stories (e.g. E4).

During this period she wrote constantly: her textbooks; school stories (in which, no doubt, her pupils and children recognized themselves more than once); *The History of Henry Milner*; *The Lady of the Manor*; about a hundred tracts for five different publishers. In these years she became famous as an Evangelical writer for children. She was invited to meet William Wilberforce (whom she found a good listener), and Elizabeth Fry. Her children grew up; Henrietta Sherwood [i.e. Mary Henrietta], the eldest of the family, married in 1826, and Mary Parsons, the elder of the orphans, in the same year. Emily, the beauty of the family, married at eighteen a local doctor, R. J. Streeten.

In 1830, Mrs. Sherwood gave up her school (which promptly failed under the management of her nieces), went with her family on a tour of the Continent, and returned in 1832 to apply herself to novel writing and story-telling.

Novelist and story-teller she remained for the rest of her life, very successful when she was writing for children such pleasant tales as *The White Pigeon* or *The Heron's Plume* or *The Useful Little Girl*; less happy when she touched with some acrimony upon politics, as in *Emancipation*, or upon Catholicism (*Julietta di Lavenza*) as a warning to the adolescent or young adult of the upper classes.

The next decade was saddened by the death of her brother in 1832, and of two daughters: Emily in 1833, and Lucy in 1835. Mrs. Sherwood rallied from these blows with greater resiliency than she had shown many years before; she had cast off the unyielding Evangelical doctrine of her Indian years. Her son was married in 1834; by 1840 he was settled in a comfortable rectory near by. Her youngest daughter, Sophia, remained at home and even after she married her brother-in-law, Dr. Streeten, they lived with the Sherwoods.

In 1849, Dr. Streeten died unexpectedly; and before the end of that year, Captain Sherwood also. Mrs. Sherwood and Sophia moved to Twickenham, where they lived quietly until Mrs. Sherwood's death in 1851. She had been writing until near the end of her life of seventy-six years.

To read Mrs. Sherwood's *Autobiography*, and Darton's *Life and Times* . . . is to feel that the thirty-five years after her return from India are but a prolonged anticlimax. She did not think so herself; nor did her Victorian readers.

'She had made the very best of all the gifts given her by God' said Mary Palgrave, one of the last editors of *The History of the Fairchild Family*, in 1902. Having jettisoned so much of Mrs. Sherwood's theory, later Victorians praised her industry and effort: these were Evangelical qualities which they valued and retained.

The Evangelical Programme

The Evangelical Movement began well before Mrs. Sherwood's birth in 1775. Between 1740 and 1790, the most famous of its early leaders, George Whitefield and John Wesley, successfully implanted it among the lower classes to which, by 1780, it appeared to be permanently restricted. For two generations the efforts of dedicated Evangelicals within the Church to bring about a spiritual awakening in upper-class circles were shrugged off, their few converts (like the Countess of Huntingdon or Sir Richard Hill) being contemptuously dismissed as eccentrics or 'enthusiasts'.

In less than forty years, however, the whole picture of religion in England had changed. By 1820 the Evangelical Movement had drawn in a wide cross-section of middle- and upper-class society, including thirty-six members of the House of Commons. It was entrenched at the University of Cambridge. The many causes supported by the Movement: the suppression of vice; the abolition of slavery; the propagation of the Gospel; missions; charities and hospitals; Sunday Schools and education; and a host of others, were zealously forwarded by innumerable societies all over the kingdom. Board and Committee members of these groups included royal dukes, representatives of all ranks of the aristocracy, writers, landowners, merchants, bankers, businessmen. Evangelicalism, by 1820 both respectable and fashionable, had drawn to itself a whole set of favourable connotations.

The Evangelical Movement is both the background and the inspiration for Mrs. Sherwood's early books for children, as it is the chief reason for the growth and success of all tract publishing in the nineteenth century. Without its moral discipline, its war against religious indifference and laxity, against ignorance, brutality, extravagance and vice, neither writer nor publishers would have had their opportunity. In turn, thanks to Mrs. Sherwood and the tract publishers, the moral and religious code and the restraints of Evangelicalism were perpetuated—dare we say, petrified?—so that they long remained a part of Victorian attitudes and assumptions. Sometimes, like seashells in a cabinet or stuffed birds in a case, they are but relics of the past, their vitality and energy long gone but their forms intact. Quite often, however, the whole outlook on life that is comprehended in the word 'Victorian' is seen to be the widely-branching top of a living tree whose root is the Evangelical Movement. From Evangelicalism stemmed a missionary fervour that was not restricted to missions, a religious zeal that overflowed into business and politics. Evangelicalism was manifest in the powerful Victorian urge to teach, preach, and learn; to better oneself and to better the lot of others. It was a driving force, a motive power, as well as a way of life, a habit of thought, and a personal discipline. Its offshoots included Millenarianism, the Tractarian movement, and the Salvation Army; what is more important in the history of children's books, Evangelicalism helped to create the Victorian belief in the family.

This change in the public attitude was largely brought about by William Wilberforce; its principles were disseminated by the educators and tract writers. Converted around 1785, Wilberforce noted in his Journal two years later:

God has set before me two great objects, the suppression of the slave trade, and the reformation of manners.

Towards these objects he worked unswervingly to the end of his life, conducting his crusade of over forty years like a modern advertising campaign, estimating the weaknesses of the worldly and indifferent, infiltrating their strongholds (by right of his own impregnable social position), propagandizing, persuading. Witty, charming, completely sincere, he gathered around him a circle of dedicated followers in London (the 'Clapham Sect'), and enlisted the aid of equally dedicated co-workers scattered over the country. Although they differed widely in background, all Evangelicals had in common an intense though narrow vision, great energy, and single-track determination. Few of Wilberforce's generation had been born to their narrow faith; turning their backs upon the broad inclusive deism or

7

the orthodox Anglicanism that went well with the rational eighteenth-century education that they had received, they deliberately chose Evangelicalism, laying upon its altar their wealth, their time, and their talents. Henry Thornton spent from one-half to four-fifths of his income upon charity; Hannah More, whose position in the Movement rivalled that of Wilberforce, had left a successful literary career in London to found Sunday Schools in the west of England and become the movement's ablest propagandist.

Evangelical success depended in large measure upon its inspired use of the printed word. The Movement had its own periodicals: *The Evangelical Magazine*; and the influential *Christian Observer*, edited by Zachary Macaulay and printed by John Hatchard whose famous Piccadilly bookshop was an outlet for all Evangelical publications. That he was also the publisher of Mrs. Sherwood's noted *The History of the Fairchild Family* and *The History of Henry Milner* is a measure of the high regard in which she was held by the Evangelicals at the time.

Sober publishing houses patronized by the Movement flourished all over the country: Rivington and Nisbet in London; Hazard of Bath; Houlston of Wellington. Since Evangelical doctrine depended upon literal acceptance of the Bible, it was essential that converts possess and read the Bible; tracts for guidance and interpretation were almost as necessary. Hence the Evangelical emphasis upon Sunday Schools, upon reading, upon the distribution of Bibles, catechisms, and tracts to young and old alike.

It was the Golden Age of the religious tract. The brilliant success of the Cheap Repository venture between 1795 and 1800 had been taken to heart by publishers as well as by dozens of earnest writers, who, in the spirit of Hannah More but usually without her skill, attempted to fill a growing demand for the printed word. Sermons and tracts designed to stimulate religion, to educate the illiterate up to a safe point, and to counteract the subversive doctrines of radical and infidel publications that the Government was failing to suppress, streamed off the presses.

It is not surprising that the Movement spread rapidly after 1800. The eighteenth century had closed in chaos. Radical and revolutionary thought undermined the traditional social structure; deism and atheism eroded religious faith. The endless war with France was attended by social unrest, economic depression and widespread misery at home; abroad, Napoleon, now in control of Europe, threatened the national existence.

When, with breath-taking confidence, the Evangelicals claimed to be able to chart a way through the universal confusion and alleviate the general distress, they found many listeners. The simplicity of their doctrines clarified moral issues, setting up unvarying standards of conduct and belief. Their chief assumption was that all issues were moral and spiritual issues. In any given situation, choice was narrowed to clearly-opposed alternatives, one pleasing to God, the other repugnant: no Debatable Land could exist between. 'I . . . may assume,' wrote Wilberforce to his son, Samuel, in 1823, 'that there are no indifferent* actions properly speaking . . . none with which religion has nothing to do.'

Such sharply-defined principles, clearly demonstrable from the Bible (the ultimate authority for the Evangelical) appeared to many a God-given clarification of the universal chaos. To subordinate all purposes to the one great religious purpose was to answer all questions, crush all doubt, reconcile all opposing viewpoints. Evangelicalism settled, for example, the vexing problem of right and station in Society: since all souls were equal in the sight of God, throughout eternity, the inequalities of bodies here on earth, being temporary, was comparatively unimportant. Slavery came under attack by the Evangelicals less for its physical miseries than for the spiritual degradation it imposed on slave and owner alike. Mrs. Sherwood makes this very point in *Babes in the Wood of the New World*. That she was not a rabid abolitionist appears from a note in her Journal:

Unjustifiable as slavery is, and wholly incompatible with Christianity, may it not be used by Almighty God for some good purpose? (*Life and Times*, p. 420)

Her tale *The Recaptured Negro* (1821) culminates in the freed slave's conversion of his pagan mother, this episode being given far more significance than the situation that

* i.e., neutral.

brought it about, for Mrs. Sherwood saw the state of bondage as a metaphor or type of the human soul's enslavement to sin rather than as a pressing social evil. At any time, a Christian slave was in better state than a free pagan.

The Evangelical Movement appealed also because of its immediacy. *Doing the next thing*, the work close to hand, was one way of restoring order in a chaotic world. For women in particular, this work was the all-important one of education: they taught the ignorant to read; bought and distributed Bibles and tracts; wrote for children, for the newly-literate, for servants and villagers. This was the work to which Mrs. Sherwood had long felt herself called. Like most ardent Evangelicals, she assumed that education on a truly religious basis would be followed by universal conversion. Unlike most, however, she went further, and asserted, like Edward Irving, that the next phase would be the Millennium—the thousand-year reign of Christ on earth. Eighteenth-century education on a rational and material basis, according to the Evangelicals, had promoted religious indifference, atheism, and revolution. They proposed to reverse this state of affairs by altering educational principles.

Eighteenth-century writers for children, Berquin, Thomas Day, Mrs. Barbauld, the Edgeworths, had advocated the Lockean virtues of tolerance, benevolence, industry and moderation, displaying man largely as a social being. Faulty social relationships were shown to have a rational cure, as, for instance, in *Goody Two-Shoes*, the tales of Maria Edgeworth, or *Sandford and Merton*. Many eighteenth-century children's tales implied a background of deism. Religion, politely acknowledged, was restricted to the Church; admirable characters, without fervour, equated social and religious duties; and the state of a man's soul was his own business. Mankind in general appeared reasonable and well-intentioned, wickedness being the result of ignorance rather than design.

This optimistic view of humanity with its underlying assumption that the redemption of society is a by-product of education was repudiated by the Evangelicals. They insisted upon individual acceptance of vital religion: its agonizing assessment of the evil at every human heart; the necessity of self-abasement and repentance which alone could culminate in the joyous assurance of salvation. They maintained, too, that without such assurance, the human soul, bedevilled by pride, vulnerable to temptation, was magnetically drawn to infidelity.

Infidelity (according to Wilberforce 'the grand peculiar evil of the present day') loomed blackly among causes for Evangelical anxiety. The classical education of the eighteenth century provided a favourable climate for its growth; its arch-priests were held to be Voltaire and Rousseau; its rites social discord, radical unrest, anarchy and revolution; its inevitable end, eternal damnation. In the Evangelical view, fast becoming the popular view, infidelity was domiciled in France. Mrs. Sherwood enthusiastically concurred in this belief, as her history textbooks make clear; and she never changed her mind.

When Martin Luther and other pious teachers had by their writings set forth the errors of popery, and opened the eyes of many to its monstrous absurdities, Satan, unwilling to lose his influence on earth, had recourse to his last and most subtle engine whereby to hold the minds of men in spiritual thraldom.

Books now becoming easy of access, and learning now taking a more universal spread, this great enemy of mankind began to fill men's hearts with a high conceit of their own mental powers; and in proportion as they exalted self, they despised their Maker. Many became infidels, despisers of all religion, vain talkers, inconsistent reasoners . . . filling the world with profane and blasphemous books. . . . The French, . . . the most daring infidels in Europe, rose up in open rebellion . . . proceeded to spread their revolutionary fury through the surrounding kingdoms, filling all Europe with war and carnage, desolation and blasphemy . . .

(*A General Outline of Profane History*, pp. 213–15)

Paradoxically, in the very circles most suspicious of French influence, the works of Madame de Genlis and Berquin were highly esteemed. Evangelicals born before the end of the eighteenth century had no desire to dislodge famous educators whose methods and principles had moulded their own habits of thought. Mrs. Sherwood's great value to the Evangelical Movement was her talent for converting the widely-accepted educational ideas of her eighteenth-century predecessors into their Evangelical equivalents. Moreover, her tales, tracts, and books (as *The History of Susan Gray* and *The History of Little Henry and his Bearer* demonstrated early on) were highly acceptable as simply-worded and attractively-presented Evangelical doctrine and were peculiarly adapted to spread and perpetuate its tenets among new readers and the very young. In Hannah More, the Evangelical Movement had found its tract writer of genius whose Cheap Repository Tracts were said to have driven out much crude and vulgar reading matter as well as neutralizing the seditious pamphlets that were circulated following the publication of Paine's *Rights of Man*. In Mrs. Sherwood and her sister, Mrs. Cameron, it found tract writers who could inculcate 'correct' doctrine from the very beginning, and train up children of all social classes in a religious habit of thought.

> 'Twill save us from a thousand snares,
>   To mind religion young;
> Grace will preserve our following years,
>   And make our virtue strong.
> (Isaac Watts: Song 12, *Divine Songs*)

The Influence of India

The copious Journal of her Indian years, supplemented by her books and tales, provides the outline of Mrs. Sherwood's Evangelical activities in four different British Bengal Army posts.* Horrified by the evidence of spiritual ignorance and physical neglect among the children of the soldiers, she sought from the first to remedy the situation. Ranged against her was the East India Company's long-standing policy of religious neutrality, which meant in practice its refusal to tolerate missionary work that might upset the native population. The apathy or opposition of Company officials was echoed by many army officers who wanted nothing of 'methodism' in the regiments. There were no schools, no teachers, often no chaplains and no services.

Nevertheless, the odds were in Mrs. Sherwood's favour. A long period of religious apathy was ending, and the East India Company policy was under attack, both from within and without. Zealous Evangelicals had been appointed as Company chaplains; Wilberforce's campaign on behalf of Indian missions made strong headway in England, even gaining the support of Company officials. Very often, the soldiers and their wives were appreciative of Mrs. Sherwood's efforts.

Her own attitude to India remained ambivalent. The beauty of the country and its Arabian Nights atmosphere appealed to her romantic temperament; the opportunity to salvage the ignorant and neglected children touched her sense of religious mission. At the same time she sorrowed bitterly over the deaths of her first two children born in

* Many of Mrs. Sherwood's tales are thinly disguised (at times, undisguised) accounts of happenings easily identified in her Journal, as for example, the story of the little chuckoor in *Juliana Oakley*; *Hoc Age*; *The Cloak*; and 'The Garden of Roses' (*The Lady of the Manor*, Vol. 4). The Evangelical prejudice against works of the imagination favoured the use of materials taken directly from life: being 'true', they were not inconsistent with the religious lesson.

India, and was haunted up to the time that she adopted the Calvinistic tenets of the Evangelical chaplains by the death, corruption, and misery that she saw all around. Grief-stricken by the deaths of her children, she turned to the rescue of regimental orphans, white and half-caste; to teaching; and to writing and translation directed to the furtherance of mission work. Her arrival having coincided with that of the 'serious' Company Chaplains, Henry Martyn, Joseph Parson, and Daniel Corrie, she made common cause with them. During these same years, Methodism was making converts in the armed forces; Mrs. Sherwood's Journal, tales, and tracts (C4, C7, and D6, for example) bear witness to the beginning of the movement that culminated years later in the figure of General Gordon.

In every post she began by setting up school, on her own veranda if need be; later Captain Sherwood got a schoolroom built or assigned. Once or twice she found a native teacher to assist in the instruction of native and half-caste children; usually a literate corporal or sergeant would work with the boys (and sometimes with illiterate soldiers who came in their spare time to learn). More children lived in the barracks than might have been expected, for the East India Company, which restricted the number of wives brought out with each regiment to ten, had no objection to native mistresses. In spite of the sickeningly high mortality rate among infants in India, Mrs. Sherwood often had more pupils than she could manage: at different times, between eighteen and sixty pupils of all ages from the three-or-four-year-old to the big half-caste drummer boy of sixteen or seventeen.

All teaching began with the Catechism, which eighteenth-century Evangelicals had revived, enlivening it by supplementary questions designed to ensure its application to everyday life and to test the child's understanding. Mrs. Sherwood wrote *Stories Explanatory of the Church Catechism* on a pattern approved by Hannah More, John Wesley, and other famous Evangelical teachers, but she greatly enlarged the proportion of enlivening material.*

* Although the earliest known edition of the *Stories* is that published by Houlston in 1817, it is probable that an edition was issued in India in 1814 from the Mission Press at Serampore, outside Company territory.

The Indian bungalow. An engraving by William Radclyffe for the frontispiece to *Stories Explanatory of the Church Catechism*, 1835. (C7)

She had found herself 'thoroughly perplexed . . . that the children could not understand any common English narrative'; and to clarify the Catechism for those who knew only the life of the Indian barracks, she strung its teachings on a thread of narrative that related every point to common incidents in the life of a child in an Indian Army post. The result is unexpectedly interesting. Between passages of stiff conventional instruction given to six-year-old Mary Mills (who is exactly contemporaneous with the little Fairchilds and very like them) appear brief, colourful vignettes of barracks life, its constant difficulties, and its coarse and ephemeral pleasures. Here as elsewhere, Mrs. Sherwood is deeply concerned with the quality of family life and the relationship of parent and child: since all her writing assumes that the life of the family parallels God's relation with man, the disintegration of the family under army conditions becomes evidence of widespread infidelity and spiritual corruption. For a modern reader, however, theology is secondary to realism in this work.

Not until Kipling brought them to life again in the 1880s were the daily happenings in the married quarters depicted with such lively detail. The lack of privacy, the constant temptation to drinking and extravagance, the easy irritability flaring up into bitter quarrels and violence are all here. Idle women with no interest but dress and gossip, and sober 'methodists' are glimpsed shopping at the *bazar* or in the 'Europe Shop', sewing and chatting, planning or giving a party, attending church or a funeral. Mrs. Sherwood, who was very well aware that children raised under barracks conditions had nothing to learn about the darker side of human life, made few concessions to sentiment in *Stories Explanatory of the Church Catechism*, and no attempts whatsoever to gloss over or ignore the sordid aspects of barracks life. A furious drunken woman hurls a stool at another: 'it was her death-blow, down she dropped, and never spoke after'. The baby lulled with gin at its own christening party dies within a few hours, and is followed by its remorseful mother. Girls, spoilt, orphaned, unsupervised, go wrong; the twelve-year-old boy (who has been given from childhood sips of his father's rum ration) steals his mother's brooch to pawn for liquor, gets drunk, and dies of sunstroke. His body, picked up in the road, lies on the bed in the barracks, 'covered with dust and dirt, the eyes were staring open and the jaws fallen'.

Such was the self-contained, completely isolated world of the Indian Army barracks in 1813. It did not change quickly. Eighty years later, Kipling dipped into it for a pair of drummer boys similar to those who awaited Mrs. Sherwood's instruction in Meerut in 1814. The result was 'The Drums of the Fore and Aft'. Half-caste regimental orphans like those whom Mrs. Sherwood sought to restore to the circle of English life suggested to Kipling his most successful creation, Kim. Kipling, however, let Kim slip back into the teeming underworld along the Grand Trunk Road, for in 1900, eager readers found that background synonymous with Romance. In 1814, it would have been interpreted as the suburbs of Hell.

Better known than the *Stories Explanatory of the Church Catechism* was Mrs. Sherwood's *The History of Little Henry and his Bearer*, the manuscript of which she had sent to England in 1813 and which was published there by Houlston a year later. It is the story of the conversion of a little boy of five or six and of his attempts (before he died at the age of eight) to convert his Indian servant—and it is a book which exerted an immediate appeal to the Evangelical conscience. Before long it had become a best-seller.

The sentiment of the book and the artful simplicity of its style attracted those who responded to the poetry of Cowper or Wordsworth, or to the novel of sentiment. In Little Henry they saw an idealized child figure, a type of innocence, whose isolation among dark-skinned Hindus made him an interesting variation of the child of nature. Converted or unconverted, he was irresistible. 'His delicate complexion, light hair and blue eyes', his quaint costume of 'panjammahs' and silver bangles on his ankles set him clearly before the mind's eye; his pathetic situation touched the heart. Although he lived in a luxurious East Indian bungalow, he was an orphan, neglected by his adoptive mother, left to the care of servants. Only his Hindu bearer, Boosy, genuinely loved him.

Boosy himself was calculated to arouse missionary concern. That a man so kind, patient and devoted as Boosy should be left an idolator, doomed through eternity, was a reproach to those who called themselves Christians. Moreover, the concrete details of the story—the Indian life and background, the journeys by 'budgerow' or 'palanquin', the plentiful sprinkling of Hindustani terms—were all in agreeable contrast to the humdrum domestic setting of the average tract. With this work, the obituary tract (which invariably stressed conversion and a Christian death) had assumed the colouring of romance. Strict Evangelicals, who saw no merit in romance, observed with approval that the book justified the recent campaign on behalf of overseas missions, and found it an emotionally convincing demonstration of vital religion.

Such books as *The History of Little Henry and his Bearer* and *Stories Explanatory of the Church Catechism* maintained a considerable circulation throughout the nineteenth century. The needs of the Evangelical chaplains who were laying the groundwork for Indian missions had set Mrs. Sherwood to work on tales illustrative of Christianity for the recent convert, and *Little Henry* was followed by *The Ayah and Lady* and *The Indian Pilgrim*, the first being mainly narrative, the second, a series of Socratic dialogues based on the Ten Commandments, and the last a simplified and Indianized *Pilgrim's Progress*. After returning to England, she wrote *The History of Little Lucy and her Dhaye* (1823); *Arzoomund* (1828); and many years later, *The Last Days of Boosy* (1842).

At all times Mrs. Sherwood was sharply aware of the predicament of the regimental orphans, many of whom were at one time or another sheltered in the Sherwoods' home.* In 1807, she took Annie Child (later adopted by her friend, Mrs. Sherer), a three-year-old whose health had been ruined by being dosed with gin. In 1808, she rescued the two-year-old Sally Pownal, 'attenuated to a degree that was fearful', a dirty little skeleton covered by a single garment. The woman who had charge of the child was deliberately starving her to death. Episodes like this help to explain why Mrs. Sherwood at this time stressed the doctrine of universal depravity.

She raised and educated Sally and another child, Mary Parsons, with her own children. For other orphans she

* She continued to contribute to their upkeep after she returned to England, and kept in touch with them for many years.

The juggernaut in action. Missionary propaganda appearing in the frontispiece to *The Indian Pilgrim*. (Engraving by William Radclyffe from a drawing by William Green.) 1818. (C9)

19

found suitable homes; and by the time she left India in 1815, she had the satisfaction of knowing that her report to the Governor-General's wife, Lady Loudoun, later Lady Moira (daughter of the Evangelical Countess of Huntingdon), had resulted in the establishment of an officially recognized orphanage for the 'motherless white girls exposed to all kinds of evil in barracks'.

Taken as a body, Mrs. Sherwood's writings at this time underscore her conviction that life in India, however attractive to Europeans, is morally disintegrating. Like Wilberforce, she also believed that:

... a military life, if not more unfavourable to religion than most others . . . is yet beset with dangers, and has some peculiar temptations, . . .

(William Wilberforce to Lady Waldegrave, 15 April 1805)

To offset the more alluring of these temptations, Mrs. Sherwood wrote a number of warning tales for young readers of the upper classes. For boys going to India as army officers or East India Company writers, there was *The History of George Desmond* (1821), a really gripping novel which has never been as well known as it deserves. Its romantic Indian setting is worked artistically into the action; the characters are convincing, though conventional; much of the apparent melodrama in the context of the times, is genuine realism. Its counterparts for girls are found in volumes I, IV, and VI of *The Lady of the Manor* and in *Ermina*.

Although she lived for over ten years in India, Mrs. Sherwood's knowledge of native life was quite superficial. For this, she is not to blame. Even had she wished to study Indian history or philosophy, she lacked the time. Restricted by her position as an officer's wife, by the regulations of the Company, and by her health and family responsibilities from having any contact with educated or high-caste Hindus, she drew her conclusions from hearsay and from what she saw about her. Thus her first-hand knowledge came from servants who were often dishonest, nurses who dosed their infant charges with opium, and from the vicious old Begum Somru. It is not surprising that, under the circumstances, she could muster no respect for Indian culture. She learned Hindustani, not to read the literature, but to be able to direct the household and carry on the simplest of Bible teachings. In spite of her fondness for allegory and symbol, she never perceived the imaginative and allegorical aspects of Hinduism: it remained for her (as for most Evangelicals) the idolatry mentioned in the Old Testament, complete with human sacrifice in the form of *suttee*. Individuals, on the other hand, particularly some of the nurses and bearers, she often liked—her picture of the faithful Boosy indicating her sincere appreciation of their good qualities.

How wide and how enduring was her influence? Undoubtedly those brought up on *The History of Little Henry and his Bearer* and the other Indian books supplied their own children in turn with them. Mrs. Sherwood had successors too, notably 'A.L.O.E.' (Charlotte Tucker), a Victorian Evangelical of the next generation whose doctrine at times resembles the hell-fire theology of Carus Wilson.

Children of literate middle-class families in particular, usually given a strict and thorough Sunday School training, must have carried through life ingrained impressions of Mrs. Sherwood's and 'A.L.O.E.'s India, and an emotional bias to match. They acquired a strong conviction of the rightness of missions, which, while it inculcated sincere concern for, and a genuine kindness towards an alien people for whom Britain was responsible, quite destroyed any latent respect for Indian tradition. The paternalism, so marked in British policy towards India, must have been partly the result of Victorian attitudes formed in the nursery.

With all its failings, the displaced East India Company had, for commercial reasons, shown consideration for Indian tradition. If it tolerated the grosser abuses of Hinduism, it never, on the social level, set up any colour bar. Nevertheless, the Evangelical missionary movement fostered a firm belief in the absolute evils of Hinduism which was perpetuated in Sunday School literature well past the middle of the century.* The moderate tone, the

* Wilberforce, whose words were almost gospel to the Evangelicals of his day, had contributed to this belief by his speeches in the House, as, for example: [cont.]

genuine affection, and the real respect that permeated the writing of scholars like Sir William Jones in the late eighteenth century, and that of Bishop Reginald Heber in 1824-5, are not much in evidence: such accounts presumably lack the dramatic contrasts and strong emotional impact favoured by the Evangelicals and their Victorian descendants.

To like, admire, or even to understand the state of affairs that one is bent upon changing, complicates the matter unbearably, and the secret of Evangelical success was simplification. Unlike the merchants of the old East India Company, the Victorian administrators were impeccably honest and deeply dedicated to the welfare of those under their rule—evangelically so. But they seldom grasped the wider economic implications of their rule; and fear of 'going native' haunted social relationships. The life of the English in India came to be hedged about with countless conventions and restrictions, taken far more seriously than they were in England. The average white woman in India lived a life resembling more closely than she realized that of the zenana she deplored. In such a social climate misunderstanding multiplied.

In 1815, however, Mrs. Sherwood faced the prospect of returning to England in good spirits.

All my Indian views and objects were then, as it were, closing upon me, not in darkness indeed, but in hope and light. Others were unfolding. High encouragement was being held out to me to write for children. So the Almighty orders our ways and gives us power to walk in them. (*Life and Times*, p. 414)

The Church Missionary Society was active in India; she had arranged accommodation for her many orphans, and been instrumental in the foundation of the new home for girls. There was great relief too in getting her surviving children out of India.

Our religion is sublime, pure and beneficent. Theirs is mean, licentious, and cruel . . . Equality . . . is the vital essence and the very glory of our English laws. Of theirs, the essential and universal pervading general character is inequality, despotism in the higher classes, degradation and oppression in the lower. (*Hansard*, XXVI, 22 June 1813)

Five months after leaving Calcutta, the Sherwoods arrived in Liverpool with a party of seven children, their own four and three orphans. She brought likewise a number of completed manuscripts, including some of those which had already been printed in India.

4

Mrs. Sherwood and the Firm of Houlston

Soon after her return to England, Mrs. Sherwood was greeted by her publisher who managed to catch her *en route* to her sister's home.

> . . . as I was going along I was met by a little, neat, cheerful man, who instantly accosted me with a very polite bow, saying, 'It is indeed a privilege to see the authoress of "Henry and his Bearer".' 'Well, to be sure,' I thought, 'and how does this person know me, and who is this very civil man, and why is he so glad to see me?' Afterwards I found that he was Mr. Houlston from Wellington, a neighbouring town, the person who had published the little book. (*Life and Times*, pp. 427-8)

The practical Edward Houlston lost no time in establishing a further business connection. Within a few months a steady stream of Mrs. Sherwood's didactic and educational works was reaching the booksellers, to the mutual advantage of writer and publisher. In the years to come, Houlston printed as many of Mrs. Sherwood's titles as all the rest of her English publishers put together.

Mrs. Sherwood herself claimed that as a result of publishing *Little Henry*, 'Mr. Houlston immediately became well known, and . . . took his place at once among superior booksellers.' The firm's anxiety to monopolize copyrights supports her statement, as does the composition of its book-lists, from 1818 to 1850 or later.

Houlston's owed its early success to its being from the beginning, like Hatchard's of London, in the Evangelical camp. Shropshire had a long history of Evangelical activity, including the ministry and writing of Richard Baxter, John Fletcher of Madeley, and the energetic Rowland Hill. The rapidly-lengthening lists of Houlston's early book advertisements which reveal the beginning of a provincial publisher also reflect the growing strength of the Evangelicals in town and country and the serious tastes of a new reading public trained by the theories of Mrs. Trimmer and Hannah More. The staple of the Wellington stock-in-trade for many years to come was the tract in all its forms, and the sermon.

The firm began about 1779 as the first Edward Houlston's bookshop in the Market Square, Wellington, passing after his death in 1800 to his widow, Frances. In 1804, she took her son, the second Edward Houlston, (1780–1840), into the twenty-five-year partnership that eventually established a successful London publishing house.*

Although in 1779 the terms 'bookseller' and 'publisher' were almost synonymous, the first Edward Houlston neither printed nor published. He eked out the proceeds of the bookshop (like the Newbery family with 'Dr. James's Powder') by sidelines such as the sale of stamps showing duty paid on hair powder, and an agency for *The Salopian Journal*. Within five years of the founder's death, however, and within a year of its formation, the firm of F. Houlston and Son was publishing. Probably the younger Edward had, until this date, been serving his seven-year apprenticeship to a printer. In 1804, he was twenty-four, married, and the father of two sons who later followed him into the business. He may have been one of the enterprising printers' apprentices, who, like John Newbery, married their masters' widows, gaining thereby wives with equipment, experience, and a knowledge of business contacts; for printing was a trade in which women took an important part, both in England and America. Whatever the facts, Mrs. Ellen Houlston, older than her husband, kept up her interest in the firm after his death in 1840.

F. Houlston and Son started in a small way, publishing sermons. There was no difficulty finding manuscripts in Shropshire: so many serious-minded clergymen were anxious to see themselves in print that a sermon or tract could be bought for a guinea or two. By the Copyright Law of 1709, purchase of a manuscript gave the printer fourteen years of copyright during which all profits accrued to him; at the end of the period, the manuscript

* See Philip A. Brown, 'Houlston's of Wellington, Shropshire', in the *Shropshire Magazine*, April 1959, pp. 15–16. A table of the changes in Houlston's trading names and addresses has been given in the present book in Appendix II, pp. 110–111.

Customers in Houlston's bookshop. An engraved frontispiece to Volume 1 of *Houlston's Series of Tracts*, c. 1835.

reverted to the author. In 1814, the copyright term was extended to cover the author's life, or twenty-eight years, whichever was the longer term. In 1815 or 1816, Mrs. Sherwood was able to reclaim the much-pirated *History of Susan Gray* and sell it, 'corrected', to F. Houlston and Son for £5, the same sum that she received for *The History of Little Henry and his Bearer* (1814); for *The Memoirs of Sergeant Dale* . . . (1815); and for *The History of Lucy Clare* (1815).

Considering the great popularity of her works, these sums seem small. Mrs. Sherwood was obviously slower than F. Houlston and Son to realize the financial possibilities of her writing. At the same time, having a number of completed manuscripts on hand, she may have decided to let them go thus cheaply, both to forward the work of the Church Missionary and the Bible Societies, and to consolidate her own growing reputation. She did not complain about her publishers, although Mrs. Cameron, their other popular tract writer, noted in her memoirs:

Had I not been ill-used about my books, and had I received what I ought to have done in common honesty, I should have been rich. . . .

(George Cameron, *The Life of Mrs. Cameron*, p. 501)

To which her son and biographer appends without explanation, 'Mrs. Cameron never received a penny for "The Two Lambs".'

Although it appears that 'F. Houlston and Son' could drive a close bargain, Edward Houlston was honest. Harriet Martineau specifically exonerated him, when after 1840, she complained that his successors (probably his widow, Ellen, and his partner, Stoneman) had reprinted her tale *The Rioters* (1827 or 1828) with 'fraudulent purpose' (evidently they had altered a tale of the 1820s to make it an anti-Chartist pamphlet). Considering it amusing, she had earlier overlooked the fact that the firm had been selling her little tracts 'and some of my larger tales . . . as Mrs. Sherwood's'.* The latter, if she knew about this trick, ignored it (unless her fifty-two-item list of her own writing

* *Harriet Martineau's Autobiography.* Edited by Maria Weston Chapman; 6th edition, Vol. I (Boston, 1885), pp. 102–5.

FRONTISPIECE.

The Chester 6th

Published by F. Houlston & Son, Wellington, Shropshire Augt 1, 1828.

W. M. Craig del.   Radclyffe Sc.

Frontispiece to *The Memoirs of Sergeant Dale* . . . (Engraving by William Radclyffe from a drawing by W. M. Craig.) 1829. (C4)

inserted at the front of Vol. I of *The Lady of the Manor* [1823] is a hint to the contrary).

After 1818, she had ceased to let Houlston engross her output. About the time that she sold *The History of the Fairchild Family* to Hatchard, Houlston suddenly raised the rate of payment, giving £25 for *The Indian Pilgrim* (1818).

By 1818 a very large proportion of the firm's output for children consisted of the works of Mrs. Sherwood and Mrs. Cameron, which were squeezing out most of the old favourites. Although Houlston's publications for adults were, from the beginning, heavily moral, didactic (and increasingly religious), children's books before 1812 showed, on the surface at least, a pleasing variety. The earliest noted so far are undated (*c.* 1809); many of them must have been exchanges from other firms. Two lists around 1809–10 (one of sixteen titles, the other twenty-three) contain in all thirty-two different books for children. Among them are half a dozen late eighteenth-century 'fairy-tales', degenerate descendants of *Euphues*, *Arcadia*, and *The Grand Cyrus*, with a dash of Perrault thrown in. A few elegant and artificial names have survived the re-writing by authors of the school of Thomas Day and the moralists; titles like *Tity and Mirtillo, or The Advantages of Affability* indicate the double descent of the tales. Laboured in style, contrived in plot, all are very much alike, their best feature being a generous supply of woodcuts large enough to lend themselves to colouring.

In pleasant contrast to these tiresome tales are such old chapbook favourites as *The History of Little Red Riding-Hood*; *Diamonds and Toads*; and *Beauty and the Beast*. Only the absence of *Cinderella* from this catalogue indicates so far that 'F. Houlston and Son' were acquainted with the strictures of Mrs. Trimmer against fairy-tales, for many of the remaining titles seem purely frivolous: *Amusing Tales*; *Christmas Amusements*; *The Cries of London*; *The Wisdom of Crop the Conjuror*; several collections of Riddles. Closer examination of surviving specimens shows that excitement and adventure are strictly controlled according to the dictates of *The Guardian of Education*. Mrs. Trimmer herself could hardly have cast a more effective damper upon the spirit of adventure than do the two tales entitled *The History of the Unfortunate But Heroic Highlander* (a dismal picture of army life); and *A Narrative of the Extraordinary Adventures of Four Russian Sailors who were cast away on the Desert Island of East Spitzbergen*. This, although 'ornamented with cuts', is guaranteed to discourage any lad from emulating Robinson Crusoe.

Tracts and sermons for children were comparatively scarce around 1809. Watts's *Divine Songs* is in the list there for sixpence; *Young Oliver, or The Thoughtless Boy* and *True Courage, or Heaven Never Forsakes the Innocent* (both of which sold for 2d.), are forerunners of the flood of tracts that was shortly to overwhelm Houlston's output for children. Prices of books range from a penny for *The Trifler, or Pretty Playthings*; *The Cries of London* and *The Parents' Best Gift* (a tract), to sixpence for the 'Fairy Tales'. Everything for children, secular or religious, is 'embellished by cuts'.

Books for younger children were generously illustrated. Most woodcuts, if unimaginative, are clear and plain; some of the better ones very attractive. Few are signed. The 'moral fairy-tales' are redeemed from utter mediocrity by agreeable oval woodcuts, often showing expressive individual faces. A signed vignette of a sinister-looking rat could be the work of William Fry, the stipple engraver, at that date probably still an apprentice. Such little woodcuts passed from firm to firm; most printers of children's books accumulated them.

Houlston's early printing compares favourably with that done by other firms of the time. Books for children were often very attractive, with legible type, wide margins, and durable paper. Mrs. Sherwood was delighted with the appearance of *The History of Little Henry and his Bearer* when she saw it in India 'in its new and elegant dress'.

Within three years there was a marked change of policy. The 1812 list (found in *Robinson Crusoe*) contains fifty books, an increase of eighteen titles. More didactic and religious books for older readers appear; among those for children— and this is *before* Mrs. Sherwood has arrived on the scene— the religious and Evangelical now predominate. Readers of the first group are offered a choice of fifteen works that included *Lord Chesterfield's Advice to his Son on Men and Women* and *Mrs. Chapone's Letters on the Improvement of the Mind*. Another twenty titles are overtly religious—tracts, sermons, or reprints of older theological works such as

Baxter's *Call to the Unconverted*. The Society for Promoting the Observance of the Christian Sabbath has obviously been active since its inception in 1809. Tracts include the familiar obituaries of the godly (two expressly directed to children); *Letters on Baptism and Confirmation*; and the Rev. C. R. Cameron's sixpenny book, *Some Account of the Nature and Effects of Thunder and Lightning* . . . Mrs. Sherwood's brother-in-law was making a serious effort to instruct the colliers in his parish of Snedshill.

In three years, books for children had been sadly reduced in number from over thirty to fifteen in all, which were, on the surface, designed to amuse as well as instruct. The novel was represented only by the innocuous *Vicar of Wakefield* and *Robinson Crusoe*. *Beauty and the Beast* is still there; some of the 'fairy-tales'; and *The History of Little Goody Two-Shoes* with its sober lesson of industry and morality. But frivolity is conspicuously absent. Gone are *Amusing Tales; Christmas Amusements; The Trifler*. Gone, too, are *The House that Jack Built; Little King Pippin*; and all the Riddle books. In their place appear Eyton's depressing *Short and Simple Annals of a Poor Child*; a book with the curious title of *The Negro: a Sketch of the Birth and Education of an American Indian* . . .; and a long assortment of sober, instructive and religious works calculated to forward the Evangelical cause.

F. Houlston and Son was, in fact, recording with barometric sensitivity the changing religious pressures of the time. Within the next year, Reginald Heber would preach in Shrewsbury his first missionary sermon for the Bible Society; and Mrs. Cameron would bring to the Wellington publisher the manuscript of *The History of Little Henry and his Bearer*. With the aid of the tract publishers, the Evangelicals were establishing their position as educators.

It is not surprising that Edward Houlston greeted Mrs. Sherwood with warmth and deference when he met her three years later, or that she continued to think kindly of the firm. Its timely printing of *Little Henry* to coincide precisely with the popular beginnings of the great missionary movement had ensured the continuing success of both writer and publisher. The widespread religious ferment explains the remarkable increase in Houlston's offerings of religious books and tracts after 1812. Their sixty-item book-list of 1818, for instance, contains fifteen titles by Mrs. Sherwood and twelve by Mrs. Cameron. Thirty-nine of the sixty titles are obviously directed to children; everything without exception is religious and Evangelical. Between 1810 and 1820, the Evangelicals had gained a large measure of control over the printed word for the young, and were preparing to raise future generations

> Of children that began to mind
> Religion in their youth.

The size of Houlston's early editions of Mrs. Sherwood's books is not known. R. D. Altick quotes seven hundred and fifty as average for an edition of a 'serious' work; the figure may be low for a children's book. Darton specifies fifteen hundred to two thousand.* There were three editions of *The History of Theophilus and Sophia* in 1818; and by 1824 the fifth edition of *The Penny Tract*, published in London for William Whittemore and Houlston, numbered five thousand.

Houlston's made extended use of the long-prevalent exchange system with other presses, thus varying stock and ensuring the widest possible distribution. The title-page of a volume of John Eyton's sermons printed in 1807 advertised that the book is sold also by Hatchard, Piccadilly; eight other firms are mentioned as well as '. . . the booksellers in Liverpool, Macclesfield, Newcastle, and Hanley, and . . . all other booksellers'. They exchanged children's books with two Derby publishers, Mozely, and Richardson of Friar Gate; in 1818 an edition of Mrs. Cameron's *The History of Margaret Whyte*, printed in Bath by Binns and Robinson, listed a number of Wellington copyrights, including *The History of Little Henry and his Bearer* and *The History of Susan Gray*; also *The History of the Fairchild Family* (printed that year by Hatchard).

These continual exchanges and the prevalence of piracy made it difficult for the writer to keep track of his works. Mrs. Sherwood, both prolific and popular, found it impossible; all she could do was come to terms with honest

---

* Altick, *The English Common Reader* (1957), p. 263, and Darton, *Children's Books in England* (2nd ed., 1958), p. 169.

publishers. With Houlston, Hatchard, and Darton, her interests were safe.

All her publishers gave Mrs. Sherwood's books the widest distribution. From 1808 until 1824–5, Houlston's London distributors were the printers with whom they exchanged titles. These included G. and S. Robinson; Scatcherd and Letterman (after 1820, Scatcherd and Co.); and John Hatchard, to whose Piccadilly shop all tracts eventually gravitated. By 1825, when the third generation of the family entered the business, the third Edward Houlston was put in charge of the Warehouse and bookshop at 65 Paternoster Row, and his younger brother, Thomas, travelled for the firm for the next ten years.

The publishing continued to expand. Houlston's kept a monopoly of Mrs. Sherwood's popular missionary tales and stories with an Indian background; and published between 1816 and 1818 several of her textbooks. A lengthening list of little tracts and chapbooks for children appeared in the Houlston book catalogues. Almost everything Mrs. Sherwood wrote at this time was conspicuously Calvinistic, Evangelical, and perfectly attuned to the needs of Clapham. Her missionary fervour did not abate for several years, and it was supplemented by her extremely successful approach to the whole subject of education.

Between 1822 and 1824, Houlston's brought out the first of several short-lived periodicals. *The Select Magazine*, inspired 'by an earnest desire to promote the welfare of the rising generation', was intended to support 'improvement in knowledge and virtue'. In prim, didactic prose, it dispensed information on such matters as the kaleidoscope, exploration, chemistry, and astronomy; and improved virtue with solemn dissertations on the Bible, and anecdotes of John Fletcher. Mrs. Sherwood supplied two serials: long, gloomy narrative tracts entitled *The Infant's Grave* and *Père La Chaise*, based on her observations of French cemeteries in 1821. (Mrs. Cameron's tales, *The Faithful Little Girl* and *The Willoughby Family*, were more cheerful.)

In 1828 came *The Gleaner*, described on its title-page as selections 'from the works of authors who have written for the benefit of their Fellow Creatures; particularly intended to furnish the working-classes with hints for the Advancement of their Comfort and Respectability'. This venture expired after one volume, probably because of the lethargy of the working-classes, no longer dependent upon tracts for knowledge or entertainment. Those who had been taught to read that they might study the Bible and gain their amusement from *The Shepherd of Salisbury Plain* or *The Dairyman's Daughter* all too often went on to study *The Rights of Man*, gaining their amusement from tales about Jack Sheppard, or Maria Monk. There was much to divert them from religion in the 1820s and 1830s: the political writings of Cobbett or William Hone; the crime broadsheets of the Catnach Press; the coarse and vital popular theatre. Current social unrest, the increase of the urban population, the agitation for mine and factory reform, all helped to destroy popular interest in the aphorisms of Benjamin Franklin (a prime favourite with Houlston's), or good advice in the style of Mrs. Trimmer and Hannah More.

Having discovered long before 1830 that a profitable business could be founded upon tracts for the masses and improving literature for the young, Houlston's was reluctant to make changes. Temporarily abandoning the uplift of the reluctant working-classes, it turned to publication in numbers for the very young with *The Nursery and Infants' School Magazine*. A monthly, edited by Mrs. Cameron who wrote most of the contents, it continued for two years, and went on after 1832 as *The Nursery Magazine*. Mrs. Sherwood, busy with Hamilton's *Youth's Magazine*, seems not to have contributed to her sister's effort.

Circumstances continued to favour the tract publishers. Until near the end of the century, the growth of population, the spread of literacy, and the concern of the educated for 'the elevation of the masses' all helped to ensure a huge and uncritical reading public. Education acts, private effort, and the work of the churches resulted in the opening of schools, Sunday Schools, and evening schools. An unprecedented demand for cheap, instructive literature of impeccable moral content had to be met by the tract societies, which in the next few decades, flourished as never before. Ironically, a good deal of Houlston's prosperity at this time came less from tracts and religious printing than from supplying textbooks and books of useful knowledge for schools. After 1850, the secularization of the schools, not really apparent before, rapidly accelerated.

Around 1830 the tracts and tales of Mrs. Sherwood and Mrs. Cameron were augmented by those of 'Old Humphrey' (i.e. George Mogridge), a highly moral author of devastating dullness, whom Houlston's shared with William Darton, the R.T.S., Nisbet, and several other publishers. The works of these three tract writers were still strongly represented in Houlston's lists of 1870, along with those of Mrs. Best and Hannah More, about four hundred and fifty separate tracts being then available. The figures are less significant than they sound, for they must be interpreted in conjunction with the vastly increased quantity of secular material offered at that date, much of it in school-books, the rest in books of general knowledge.

Before 1870, religion had lost its grip upon education. Children's books were channelled into two streams: the practical and the amusing. Determined as ever 'to promote the welfare of the rising generations', Houlston's elected to supply the practical. The firm published little fiction except in the narrative tracts and the works of Mrs. Sherwood and similar safe writers, but it made much of useful knowledge for adults: *Enquire Within Upon Everything*, for example, was theirs (at its 378th thousand in 1868), and the twenty-four other volumes of what they called 'this series of Popular and Valuable books'. A dull and domestic periodical, *The Family Friend*, ran for some years after it began in 1849.

Meanwhile, the work of Mrs. Sherwood, Mrs. Cameron, Hannah More, and other Evangelicals was endlessly reprinted and widely circulated. But it was by the 1870s largely confined to Sunday reading and to those libraries put together wholesale for schools, churches, and institutions.

On behalf of Sunday reading (for which by 1860 a whole body of specially written literature existed to keep young minds off worldly affairs on the first day of the week), Houlston's kept all the old copyrights in print. In 1866, thirty-four titles of the Copyright Edition Illustrated of Mrs. Sherwood's works were available, many with pleasing

Kronheim frontispieces. They included a three-volume *Roxobel*; and *The History of George Desmond* which, after fifty years, had ceased to be anonymous. All the original Evangelical works of 1814 and 1820 were still there; chapbooks and tracts could be supplied in quantity on demand.

The firm's monopoly of Mrs. Sherwood's religious and missionary tales had lapsed on her death in 1851. Other publishers (notably Milner and Sowerby) had encroached; and the 1860s and 1870s saw a great reprinting of Mrs. Sherwood's work for Sunday Schools.

In 1906, Houlston's sold out to Madgwick; around 1910 the firm disappeared. *The History of Little Henry and his Bearer*, the book that had made the fortune of the firm, has survived it. In its century of publishing life, Houlston's had first made Mrs. Sherwood famous, and had in turn, been nourished by her fame. But the Victorian insistence upon useful knowledge was fundamentally antagonistic to the original idea behind tract printing, and secular education, fitting itself to an industrialized world, shook off the last vestiges of Evangelical influence about the time of the First World War. With them went the works of Mrs. Sherwood.

5

Evangelical Education

A very different situation had prevailed around the time of the Napoleonic Wars and immediately afterwards. The Evangelicals were rapidly gaining control of education and of much publication for the young.

Like her predecessors, Hannah More and Mrs. Trimmer, Mrs. Sherwood had tackled the problem of education Bible and tract in hand. Unlike them, however, she was at heart a Romantic; being also a novelist, she had at her finger-tips the fictional elements of sentiment and romance. Her writing had the charm of novelty at a time when the mass of religious tracts followed a conventional and outworn pattern. No change could be made in the essential lesson of the tract; but Mrs. Sherwood could supply picturesque, and often original, background and spin it out into narrative, as she did in *The Orphans of Normandy* and *Theophilus and Sophia*.

She was not an original thinker, but in 1817 originality in education was at a discount. Dissenters and Established Church authorities (whether Evangelical or not) agreed that education should subserve religion. Wesley had been emphatic upon this point; Mrs. Trimmer made it central to her system. On her return from India, Mrs. Sherwood made no attempt to break new ground in matters of education; following current practice, she built on foundations already laid, altering and imitating earlier didactic and educational material, and adding the one thing needful.*
Moral tale; allegory; dialogue; question and answer; child and mentor; the academy—all the familiar devices reappear in her works with but one essential difference: for eighteenth-century dependence upon reason, Mrs. Sherwood substitutes the Evangelical assumption that all learning is of necessity rooted in and directed towards

---

* It was the great age of imitation. Everybody who wrote a primer copied Mrs. Trimmer. Mangnall's *Questions* was another popular model. Mrs. Sherwood borrowed in all directions. Carus Wilson helped himself to Berquin's title, *The Children's Friend*, for the gloomiest of all Evangelical publications for the young.

religion. Education thus becomes preparation for eternity; rational and moral elements are subordinated to lessons of faith, resignation, and implicit obedience to the will of God; and the material concerns of everyday life are thinned out.

Her first attempt to banish worldly things had taken place in India and resulted in two long religious allegories based on *The Pilgrim's Progress*. *The Infant's Progress*, an expanded tract in allegorical form, dealt with life and death. Written in 1807/8, it presents three young pilgrims of nine, eight, and seven. The theological balance is tipped in favour of Calvinism by the addition of In-bred Sin to the cast of characters, an infant demon who complicates the journey by inciting Humble Mind, Playful and Peace to quarrel, disobey, overeat, or indulge in Filthy-Curiosity. Some young readers are said to have enjoyed his performance more than the hard-won spiritual victory of his little victims. The second allegory, *The Indian Pilgrim*, was written in 1811/12 on the suggestion of the chaplains, Henry Martyn and Daniel Corrie, for use with native converts. Both books, printed by Houlston's after Mrs. Sherwood's return from India, were, by reason of their novelty of setting and sentiment, immediately popular, and remained approved Sunday reading for the rest of the century.

Although she wrote no more long allegories after 1812, Mrs. Sherwood produced at intervals allegorical tracts such as *The Golden Clew*, *The Shepherd's Fountain* and *The Mourning Queen*. Her fondness for figurative style and language appears too in the innumerable types and emblems which crowd her pages; and in the central metaphors of her longer works such as *The History of the Fairchild Family*.

After 1817, her reputation as a children's writer of 'correct' (i.e. Evangelical) principles grew.* She omitted no cause dear to the Movement: the need for missions; charity; Sunday Schools; the evils of slavery. The content of her textbooks indicates that here the Bible Society, the Society for the Propagation of the Gospel, and the question of Sabbath observance took priority.

* For a brief discussion of Evangelical vocabulary see the note at the end of this chapter.

The advertisement to the *Introduction to Astronomy Intended for Little Children* (C6) makes every effort to keep science in its place.

In the astronomical lessons, every thing difficult and abstruse has been omitted, as far as it was possible . . .; and such parts of Scripture as have been found applicable, have been introduced, in order that in every day's lesson, some little portion of Scripture might be impressed upon the mind of the learner . . .

Five years later she set about disciplining other fields of knowledge. The section devoted to printing in *A General Outline of Profane History* is directed only to the printing of the Bible; and the Preface to *A Chronology of Ancient History*, a book which attempts to trace all the principal nations of the earth back to the time of Noah, explains that since her Indian experiences, the author had hoped to 'establish her heathen pupils in the persuasion of their being connected in such a bond of relationship with their Christian brethren, as might prepare their hearts, under the divine blessing, to partake with them of the promises of the gospel . . .'. Obviously the intent of these (as indeed of all Evangelical texts) was to offset the deistical tendency to consider knowledge an end in itself.

Of far greater significance was her revision of a justly famous child's book of the previous century: Sarah Fielding's *Governess, or Little Female Academy*, which she brought into conformity with Evangelical belief. Raising its low-keyed and reasonable tone to one of high-pitched religious exhortation, and altering the tales accordingly, she put the book out in 1820 under her own name, thereby squeezing the original out of the educational picture until it was resurrected by Charlotte Yonge in 1870.

This model of the academy, its original elements of kindly authority and disciplined order stiffened by a large infusion of Evangelical doctrine, she reproduced in various forms for the rest of her life, her many school stories including such titles as *The Broken Hyacinth, Caroline Mordaunt, Clara Stephens, The Flowers of the Forest, The History of Henry Milner, The Two Sisters* and *Boys will be Boys*. The fictional academy was a classical device, long accepted as

FRONTISPIECE.

Frontispiece to Mrs. Sherwood's first revised edition of Sarah Fielding's *The Governess*, 1820 (Engraving by William Radclyffe from a drawing by William Green.) (C13) peculiarly suitable for the instruction of youth and it had many attractions for an author bent on religious education. There was the satisfaction of purifying and adapting to religious ends a notable device of the infidel philosophers. Then, too, the academy was a surrogate for the family, which, to Mrs. Sherwood, is the type of man's relationship with God.

> . . . the parental feelings are the type, imperfect indeed, of the Divine love, whilst the less disinterested, that of the child for the parent, is the emblem of that of the creature in the most exalted state. (*Life of Mrs. Sherwood . . .*, p. 514)

The great overriding metaphor of all her work is the representation of divine order by the harmonious family relationship (invariably set in its own pastoral Eden). By logical extension, in which she is as adept as any eighteenth-century moralist, she progresses to the place of the child in the cosmic order. Her influence upon the domestic pattern of Victorian life can hardly be overestimated. No writer made it clearer to her readers that the child who is dutiful within his family is blessed in the sight of God; or stressed more firmly that family bonds are but the earthly and visible end of a spiritual bond running up to the very throne of God. Neglectful, harsh, or cruel, as a parent might be, children in Evangelical belief were still under heavenly command to be dutiful. Indissolubly linked to the divine order, the situation on earth was not to be judged on appearances.

The academy in Mrs. Sherwood's writing is second only to the family as the type of heavenly order, lending itself similarly to variations upon the Fifth Commandment. She pictures three kinds of schools, touching lightly upon the fashionable establishment such as that which produced Caroline Mordaunt, and the pretentious and trivial board-ing-school, of whose pupils vulgar Miss Kitty of *Intimate Friends* is a sample. Her ideal academy is modelled upon Sarah Fielding's, a little school with six or eight pupils and a domestic atmosphere. Older girls in sisterly fashion help to instruct the little ones; curriculum is slightly more specific than that offered by Mrs. Teachum, being rather like Mrs. Sherwood's own, where:

> The young Ladies are taught—
>
> ENGLISH   HISTORY
> FRENCH   GRAMMAR
> ASTRONOMY   WRITING
> GEOGRAPHY   CIPHERING
>
> And the Learned Languages if required.
>
> (Mrs. Sherwood's *Prospectus*)

Most of the governesses, like Mrs. Teachum, are mild, motherly, and amiable. The strictest of these academies was the first, Mrs. Sherwood having revised *The Governess* during her strongly Calvinistic period. All the excellent ladies (and a number of the pupils) hold Mrs. Sherwood's own strong opinions upon doctrine and show her fondness for emblems and morals.

> . . . before we dismiss this story, shall we not try to draw some profitable moral from it? Who is this chuckoor story like, and what lesson of wisdom does it contain?'
>
> 'I know, my dear aunt,' said Anna, . . . 'it is like mine—like your poor niece's, my dear aunt. I was left destitute and helpless when a very little baby . . . and you became my dear honoured mother—you took me into your bosom—you guarded and protected me . . . and now in this sweet retirement, I am daily enjoying every temporal comfort and every spiritual advantage which can be partaken on earth. The little chuckoor is not capable of thanking his Maker for all that he has done for him, but I, with the divine help, will thank him—I will praise him—I will bless him, and that for ever, for all his unspeakable mercies.
>
> (*Juliana Oakley*, pp. 70–71)

Like her fellow-writer for the young, Elizabeth Sandham in *The School Fellows* (1818), Mrs. Sherwood evidently felt that the school story gave opportunity for depicting the world in miniature, and '(displaying) a variety of characters, not difficult to be met with, as examples and warnings'. The pupils in her academies are sufficiently varied to allow for conflicts of opinion; their behaviour demonstrates that, as Wilberforce expressed it, 'there are no indifferent actions'. Jealousy, spite, vanity are the chief faults displayed, bringing about their own punishment in the form of remorse and regret.

Sarah Fielding was not the only one of her eighteenth-century predecessors to be raided by Mrs. Sherwood on behalf of Evangelical education. She drew very heavily upon Madame de Genlis, whom she did not hesitate to criticize in *Caroline Mordaunt* for the Spartan rigours of her regime. *The Lady of the Manor*, as its Victorian critics complained, was cast in the mould of *Veillées du Château*, which it also echoes in the French settings of many stories. The attacks upon Voltaire in this book, as in several others, and the sensational theme of young women being coerced into convents can be paralleled in the writings of Madame de Genlis as well as in her memoirs.

Such close resemblances are not always the results of deliberate imitation. The two women were similar in temperament; both strong-minded, dominating the men to whom they were attached; both devout, defending religion and abhorring atheism. Both advocated the simple, rural life, and emphasized the corruption underlying a sophisticated society. Like Madame de Genlis, Mrs. Sherwood wrote in favour of the adoption of children and herself adopted several orphans.

The work of Arnaud Berquin, moral rather than religious, did not lend itself so readily to Mrs. Sherwood's shaping hand. Nevertheless, Berquin's habitual pattern of small domestic situations acted out by children under the eye of parents or fellows, appears constantly in Mrs. Sherwood's tales about the very young. The chapter headings of *The Looking-Glass for the Mind* (1787) have a family resemblance to those of the early books of *The History of Henry Milner*; many episodes in *Henry Milner*, Part I, are much like tales in Berquin's book. In *L'Ami des Enfants*, (1782–3), on which *The Looking-Glass* was based, the tale 'Mutual Friendship' deals with four children, who, having quarrelled, are ordered by their governess each into a different corner of the room for the rest of the day. Horribly bored with their isolation as anger cools, they plead for different treatment, and are gently reminded of their need for each other.

From this time, no idle peevishness troubled their harmonious intercourse; and instead of bickerings and discontents among them, nothing was seen but mutual condescension. . . .

(*The Children's Friend*, Vol. III)

43

When this episode is set beside Mr. Fairchild's displaying the gibbeted murderer to his quarrelsome children, the greatest difference between the moral and the Evangelical philosophies of education becomes clear. It is also obvious that of the two writers, Mrs. Sherwood knew more about real children.

With Mrs. Barbauld, Mrs. Sherwood shared a love of nature and a strong sense of natural beauty, but there is little indication that she drew from Mrs. Barbauld's works. Miss Edgeworth's view that it was not right 'to introduce the awful idea of God's superintendence upon puerile occasions'* was, to Mrs. Sherwood, the beginning of infidelity: Evangelicals knew that *all* occasions were equally important in the sight of God. Although Mrs. Sherwood herself enjoyed Miss Edgeworth's books, her dislike of Rousseau's theories, and her personal knowledge of the Edgeworths' circle of friends at Lichfield made the Edgeworth system of education suspect. She never altered her opinion of it; and beginning in 1822 she counter-attacked with *The History of Henry Milner*.

Mrs. Trimmer, in fact, seems to have been the only one of Mrs. Sherwood's predecessors to meet with her complete approval. Mrs. Trimmer had praised *The History of Susan Gray* (1802), in *The Guardian of Education* (1802); Mrs. Sherwood returned the compliment some years later when she used Mrs. Trimmer's *Oeconomy of Charity* as the basis for a story in *The Lady of the Manor*, Vol. I (1823); and again when Emily Fairchild selects *The History of the Robins* to read for pleasure in Book II of *The History of the Fairchild Family*.

A Note on Evangelical Terminology
Like all Evangelicals of the day, Mrs. Sherwood appropriates certain terms of favourable connotation and restricts their use to her own belief. Only members of the Movement could be described as *sincere*, *religious*, *serious* or (a cause of offence to those outside the Movement but not outside the Church) *Christian*. The person who was *gay* or who could be accused of *levity* was by implication in

* Mrs. S. C. Hall in *The Art Journal*, as quoted by Sarah J. Hale in *Lessons from Women's Lives* (1875), p. 154.

44

spiritual danger. *Correct*, as adjective and as verb, was a favourite term with Mrs. Sherwood who used it to mean '*brought into* (or *to bring into*) *conformity with Evangelical belief*'. Thus, at various times, she 'corrected' Sarah Fielding's *Governess*, the ideas of her predecessors, her father's novel, her own *The History of Susan Gray* and *The History of the Fairchild Family*, and—to its detriment—her charming little *Primer* (C16). What she corrected she would have described as *dark*, or *defective*, in doctrine.

Pious appears constantly in a wholly favourable connotation. Little Arthur has a '*pretty* book about *pious* children who have devoted themselves to the service of God'. The many *pretty books* or *pretty stories* of this time (including those three samples given in the first part of *The History of the Fairchild Family*) indicate that *pretty* is synonymous with *suitable for religious instruction*.

6

Mrs. Sherwood's Style as a Writer for Children

A discussion of the facsimiles

To inculcate sound religious belief painlessly *The Little Woodman and his Dog Caesar*, a tale for the very young of all classes, could hardly have been bettered. Outlasting for generations the textbooks and the revised *Governess*, it remained, like *The History of the Fairchild Family*, in print until the present century.*

Seldom has so much essential tract material been so sensationally presented for children. Touching by implication on many of the commandments, the tale stresses faith and prayer and shows the relationship between them. In terms that children understand (for Mrs. Sherwood never forgot how children think and feel), every incident demonstrates answer to prayer: Little William's finding scraps of food and a spring of water; the dog's arrival in time to save him from the wolf and to drag him from the water; the light in the cottage window to indicate the right path. The faith of adults, too, is shown to be justified as the prayers of the woodcutter and the grandmother are answered. As in all Mrs. Sherwood's works, the re-establishment of family harmony parallels the restoration of religious faith.

It illustrates also the Evangelical rule of duty to God and duty to child, parent, and brother. Mrs. Sherwood plays no favourites: duty is as strictly imposed on parent as on child. The woodcutter's devout mother had failed to discipline her son:

She often used to say, 'I loved your father so foolishly that I never corrected him, so God corrected me. But I will love you,

* Isabella Gilchrist mentions it in 1907 (*Life of Mrs. Sherwood*. London, Robert Sutton):

'. . . *Henry and his Bearer, The Fairchild Family, The Lady of the Manor, The Little Woodman and his Dog Caesar*, are now the best known . . .'

LITTLE WILLIAM JOINING HIS DYING FATHER IN PRAYER.

Woodcut by J. Knight from *The Little Woodman and his Dog Caesar* (Parlour edition), London
?1864.

47

my little grandson, with a wiser love, and will not fail to punish you when you are naughty.'

As a result of this misplaced tenderness, the woodcutter himself was:

. . . so sinful as to neglect to teach his children to serve God . . . [He] neither thought of his Saviour nor of his poor mother's instructions, until God brought him to reflection by a dreadful accident. . . .

Repenting on his death-bed, he does his best to teach Little William 'whose heart was not yet grown hard, like the hearts of his brothers'. William, who is corrected by his grandmother, grows up pious, raises a God-fearing family, and is able to solace and instruct his remorseful brothers. With the same unrelenting logic displayed in *The History of the Fairchild Family* and the tracts of the period, Mrs. Sherwood makes consequences follow inexorably upon action: everyone reaps what he sows.

In its simplest form, the child's duty, as demonstrated by Little William, is implicit obedience, that foundation-stone of Evangelical doctrine that could not be laid too early. Obedience, it must be remembered, was instilled less as a convenience to parents than as a prerequisite to faith.

Our natural parents are the same to us, in our infancy, as God and our Church are to the believer in and after life; and hence the little child who is taught to love, honour and obey his parents, to trust in them, and submit wholly to their wills, is as well prepared, as sinful man can be, for that state of dependence on his heavenly Father, in which all human wisdom doth consist. (*The Father's Eye*, 1830, p. 6)

In contrast to Little William, the woodcutter's older sons, thieves, drunkards, neglectful of their dying father and cruel to William, display the awful results of infidelity. Upon the Spiritual Barometer—that useful guide for Evangelicals reproduced opposite—their conduct registers but a single notch above death and perdition.

The Cardinal Points on the Spiritual Barometer.

70 GLORY
Dismission from the body.
60 Desiring to depart, to be with Christ.
Patience in tribulation.
Glorying in the Cross.
50 Ardent love to the souls of men.
Following hard after God.
Deadness to the world by the Cross of Christ.
40 Love of God shed abroad in the heart.
Frequent approach to the Lord's Table.
Meetings for prayer and experience.
30 Delight in the people of God.
Looking to Jesus.
20 Love of God's house and word.
Vain company wholly dropp'd.
Daily perusal of the Bible with prayer.
10 Evangelical light.
Retirement for prayer and meditation.
Concern for the soul. Alarm.

0 INDIFFERENCE
Family worship only on Sunday evenings.
Private prayer frequently omitted.
Family religion wholly declined.
10 Levity in conversation.
Fashions, however expensive or indecent, adopted.
20 Luxurious entertainments.
Free association with carnal company.
30 The Theatre, Vauxhall, Ranelagh, etc.
Frequent parties of pleasure. House of God forsaken.
Much wine, spirits, etc.
40 Love of Novels, etc.
Scepticism—Private prayer totally declined.
Deistical company prized.
50 Parties of pleasure on the Lord's Day.
Masquerades, Drunkenness—Adultery.
Profaneness, lewd songs.
60 Infidelity—jesting at religion.
Sitting down in the chair of the scorner.
70 Death.
PERDITION

[This convenient measure of the spiritual state is found in *The Evangelical Magazine* for the year 1800. It is reproduced in full in Paul Sangster's *Pity My Simplicity* (Epworth, 1963), p. 147.]

For readers raised upon the obituary tract, *The Little Woodman and his Dog Caesar* contained all the familiar elements: beginning with the illness, repentance, and death of the woodcutter, it ends with the repentance of the six wicked brothers. Appropriate comment and scriptural quotations are embedded in the story, and since its religion is at all times the simplest Bible Christianity, the book could be held to support the work of the Bible Society.

The Little Woodman and his Dog Caesar seems to have passed without comment from the Evangelical reviewers, who often qualified their praise of Mrs. Sherwood's works with a caution against her fondness for narrative. Perhaps the Biblical parallels in *The Little Woodman and his Dog Caesar* disarmed criticism. A child could detect many resemblances to the story of Joseph and his brethren; and William forgiving his starving brothers and providing for them also brings to mind the parable of the Prodigal Son. *The Pilgrim's Progress*, too, is brought to mind; William must follow a path, cross a stream, knock insistently upon a door.

None of these borrowings from religious sources is made too obvious, for Mrs. Sherwood (whose latent romanticism was reviving) clothed them ingeniously in the chapbook trappings of the tales of her youth. Little William, like heroes of folk-tale, is the youngest child of seven, and rejected by his brothers. His adventures are narrated in a series of short, dramatic episodes, each arising logically from the one before it, each communicating a single sharp emotion skilfully underscored by visual detail. The death of the woodcutter gains added pathos from the contrasting behaviour of his children.

. . . When the wood-cutter lay sick upon his bed, William sat on his bolster, and watched beside him, and was always ready to bring him every thing that he wanted . . . and Caesar lay at his feet . . .

But the older sons:

... came in with a deer which they had killed in the forest, and a
cask of brandy which they had bought from some travellers ...
making a great fire in the hut, they roasted part of the venison,
and opened the cask of brandy. They took no notice of their
poor dying father ...

Suspense, of the kind children understand, is provided
by the plotting of the brothers and by their preparation for
the journey. The reader (or listener) knows, though
William does not, why Caesar is dragged away and locked
up, and what William's fate could be. His concern for
Caesar in their absence, and the dreadful inequality of the
visible forces of good and evil add pathos.

The details of the three-day journey are cunningly varied,
as in the preparation for the appearance of the wolf. One
night they light a fire 'for fear of wild beasts'; the next
night the beasts becomes 'wolves ... howling and baying';
and two nights later the terrified Little William sees before
him 'two glaring eyes' and hears 'a snarling noise' just
before the long-dreaded wolf is routed by the brave
Caesar.

When on the morning of the fourth day Little William
awakes to find himself deserted, he becomes one of the
army of the lost children of folk-tale and legend who drift
forever through the eternal Wood, familiar figures of
nursery-lore whose potent appeal never lessens. Mrs.
Sherwood, who was haunted by memories of two little
graves in India, and whose heart was tender to all children
orphaned, abandoned, or abused, quite literally could not
bear the thought of lost children. Over and over again she
rewrote the pathetic tale of the lost Babes of the Wood,
giving it every time a happy ending. Children may die in
her stories: death is part of the human condition. But they
do not disappear without trace—lost, strayed, or stolen,
they are either restored to their parents or taken into a
secure home. Thus the Gipsy Babes (C26) after their
sojourn in the wilderness come again to the boy's home,
and his thankful parents adopt the little gipsy girl who
accompanies him. The Babes in the Wood of the New
World (C34) caught in the terrors of a slave rebellion, are

rescued. Little Edwy, Little Flory, Little Reuben are found; the Little Beggars are taken in by friendly neighbours; Little Sally, Little Martin, the Orphan Boy (C47) and many others find not only shelter but loving kindness.

In obedience to her prevailing metaphor, every lost child in Mrs. Sherwood's tales is also a type of the Lost Sheep or Lamb—errant humanity sought by God the Father, or Christ the Shepherd. Little William, finding his grandmother, is assured of being taught to love God, and Jewish Tamar, kidnapped by gipsies, is providentially abandoned at Shanty's forge, later to learn and act upon the principles of Christianity (H5).

Mrs. Sherwood presents her lost children with much of the art of the Gothic novelist. Hers is the timeless and universal wood that stretches from the Castle of Udolpho to the cottage of Red Riding Hood's grandmother (or, in this instance, of William's grandmother). Its territory constantly increases; it has no ordinary inhabitants. Even Little William is a variant of Everychild, and it is no accident that his name, 'William', means 'resolution'. Within the borders of the Wood exist a multitude of beings at once strange and familiar—ghosts, goblins, fairies, Red Cross Knight, Robin Hood, or Tom-Tit-Tot. Its sinister shadows and dangerous corners are offset by its pleasant havens; Mrs. Sherwood, who loved the novels of Mrs. Radcliffe, Mrs. Inchbald and Clara Reeve, knew it well.

Nevertheless, she briskly rejected the traditional monsters of the Wood. Indeed, in her spiritual drama, dragon or giant would have been anticlimactic: the evil at the human heart as displayed in the conduct of William's six brothers was sufficiently terrifying. It is interesting that, as early as 1818, although she could well have sent the six wicked brothers to dangle on that gibbet that she had herself erected among the terrors of the Wood, she did not do so. They survive to repent: Mrs. Sherwood was already seeking that kindlier faith that within a few years replaced Evangelical Calvinism in her works. Probably inspired originally by tales of Robin Hood, the wicked brothers have been carefully stripped of his glamour; like similar characters in the tracts of Hannah More, they are ordinary poachers who could earn an honest living but elect not to do so.

The Little Woodman and his Dog Caesar had plenty of excitement and emotion for children of Little William's age (which is five) and those a little older. The loss of his father, the unkindness of his brothers, the parting from his dog, and the terrors of loneliness, darkness, and fear, make an unnerving sequence which is neatly balanced by the parallel build-up of consolations. There could be no happier ending after cold and dark and fear:

... they saw, not a hundred yards before them, a cottage standing in a garden: for the light from the window was so strong, that they could see even the garden-rails and the little wicket. . . .

'Come in, then, come in,' said the old woman, opening her door.

'Come in, poor little fellow: you and your dog are both welcome.'

There is a warm fire, a cat on the hearth, light and welcome and food. The wounded Caesar is fed and given a spot to sleep, Little William is kissed and comforted, and an abundance of homely detail makes the incident a true homecoming.

'Poor little boy!' said the old woman, 'if I can make you happy, you shall be happy.' And she kissed his little wet cheek.

Then she put some milk upon the fire, with bread broke into it; and while it was warming she took off William's wet clothes, and having washed the dust and mire from him, she wrapped him in a blanket, and laid him in her bed, hanging his clothes to dry against the morning: after which she brought him the warm milk and bread . . .

This is a home indeed: an oasis of warmth and light and welcome in the Dark Wood, a comforting adult to close the door against the cold and the wolves, lasting reassurance and affection.

No doubt the excellent Caesar contributed largely to the popularity of the tale. Mrs. Sherwood liked all animals, and dogs and cats in particular. Caesar was but one of several friendly and helpful dogs like Poor Burruff (C62) who saves his little master from a cobra, and Nero who brings little Reuben away from the river and back to his home (H25).

Most of her dogs are based on her own recollections of a real Caesar, 'the poor, large, yellow dog which had been the companion of our childhood'; it appears from her Journal that she would have liked to believe that animals had souls.

Throughout the century *The Little Woodman and his Dog Caesar* was constantly reprinted without alteration. Once only, it was rewritten, with a thoroughness amusingly reminiscent of Mrs. Sherwood's own efforts with *The Governess*. In 1863-4, Mrs. Mary Sewell (the mother of Anna Sewell and generally regarded at the time as the poetess of children's tract literature), took it in hand and published *The Little Forester and his Friend. A Ballad of the Olden Time.* Observing in the Preface that she was indebted to Mrs. Sherwood for the principal incidents in the ballad, she continued:

. . . it has been thought, that were the little hero of 'the olden time' clothed in a new dress, he would fully maintain his favour and popularity with the present generation . . .

It is precisely the argument used by Mrs. Sherwood's editors to excuse her tampering with Sarah Fielding's book. The result of Mrs. Sewell's literary pilfering was a 'ballad' of three hundred and seventy-three of the doggerel four-line stanzas that were her speciality. Padding the sparse lines of the tale heavily with description of nature, and inflating the sentiment with tear-laden clichés, Mrs. Sewell altered the story out of all immediate recognition.

> His brothers all were hardy men
>   When he was but a child;
> And thus he grew a lovely flower,
>   And blossomed in the wild.
>
> His eyes were darker than the blue
>   That shades the evening light,
> His cheeks were like the heather bell
>   Upon the mountain height.
>
> His gentle heart was good and true,
>   His simple words were kind,
> A better little lad than he
>   But seldom might you find.

She added detail wherever possible, leaning heavily on rhetorical devices dear to weaker Victorian writers. 'I cannot tell you the names of the six elder sons' Mrs. Sherwood had said, getting down with admirable brevity to the adventures of Little William. But Mrs. Sewell could, and did, twice, at length:

> Could that be ruthless Dagobert?
> Now crippled, old, and lame?
> Wild Cerdic this? stern Hugo that?
> All crouching down with shame.
>
> And could that be his brother Guy?
> Who made the forest ring;
> And that he Sweyn? whose bushy locks
> Once matched the raven's wing.

The outline of the story as she tells it is substantially the same, but, as in late Victorian revisions of *The History of the Fairchild Family*, the proportions of the tale have been destroyed. Mrs. Sherwood's carefully maintained balance between family and religious duty disappears with Mrs. Sewell's deletion of many religious passages and her dropsical inflation of the sentiment surrounding the family.

This 'ballad', like others by Mrs. Sewell, seems to have thrived for the next thirty years, existing beside the many new editions of the original tale which remained a favourite.

Whereas *The Little Woodman and his Dog Caesar* displays Mrs. Sherwood's ability to make Evangelical theory both exciting and convincing, her chapbook reproduced here shows why her influence was so strong outside the Sunday School. It represents that 'vigorous, cheerful, affectionate spirit' which even the Victorian reviewer who condemned her religious teachings was quick to admit,* and reflects something of her acute understanding of children's feelings, her ready sympathy, and her pleasant humour.

Like so many of the writer's stories, *Soffrona* and some of her other little chapbooks probably began as bedtime

* *The Living Age*, Vol. 43, p. 362 (taken from *The Christian Remembrancer*).

tales. A natural story-teller of great talent, Mrs. Sherwood had from childhood collected or composed stories to amuse her little sister; in later years, her Sunday scholars and her own children were ready listeners. Her Journal describes typical evenings at Wick during the winter of 1817 after the return from India:

... The little ones had colds and chilblains, and I could not go out. In the dusk I always was with them in that room. I used first to tell them a story from my own head, as we gathered round the fire, and then a merry tune was played and they all danced. . . . It mattered not if it were the same air and the same figure every evening. . . . Some of these stories were afterwards written down and have found their way into print, where I trust they have pleased other little ones. . . . (*Life and Times*, p. 439)

Among these tales may well have been *The Little Woodman and his Dog Caesar*, as well as many of the chapbooks.

Yet another source for these little tales may have been Mrs. Sherwood's recollection of stories told to her when she was young. For instance, she attributed *Little Robert and the Owl*, one of the chapbooks in series with *Soffrona*,* to one of her father's curates, a distant cousin, Mr. Nash, whom Dr. Butt's children called Uncle Robert.

... It was a happy day when he was seen coming across the park in his great bushy wig, his shovel hat, his cravat tied like a King William's bib, his cheap great-coat, and his worsted spatter-dashes.† When this figure arose above our horizon (however remote) my joy, and that of my brother, was excessive, for he was the man of all others to delight children. As soon as it was dark in a winter evening, I took my place on his knee, and calling him Uncle Robert, begged for a story. Again and again I had heard the same, but the oft-told tale never tired; he told of dogs who were supposed to have been spirits, and who were always seen in the rooms of certain persons when any of the family were about to die, and of other marvels of the same kind; added to which he could bark like a dog himself, and grunt like a pig, and play tricks with cards . . . he will not be forgotten so long as

* Included by E. V. Lucas in his collection of *Old Fashioned Tales*, 1905.
† Spatter-dashes: long leggings or gaiters to protect the wearer from mud and water splashed up by the horses.

'Robert and his Owl' and 'Henry Milner' are to be found in the libraries of little children. (*Life and Times*, p. 28)

Mary Butt was probably no more than four when she heard this tale, and Mr. Nash's story of the faithful dog (*The History of Henry Milner*, Part I).

Soffrona and her Cat Muff was published only ten years after *The Little Woodman*, but it exists in a different world, moving between a happy home guided by a loving mother, and a little cottage with a kind old woman, and a cat on the hearth. The wood that must be crossed is a delightful place where children can find:

. . . snail-shells, and painting-stones, and wild strawberries, and bilberries, and walnuts, and hazel nuts, and beautiful moss, and many kinds of flowers; and there they heard birds sing— cuckoos, and linnets, and blackbirds, and thrushes; and saw beautiful butterflies with gold and purple plumes, and dragon- flies, whose wings look like fine silk net.

It is not quite free of harm; for the cruel, mischievous boys come to the brook to drown the stolen kitten, which is rescued by the little girls, Soffrona and Sophia.

Each small episode is delicately picked out in detail: the little walks through the wood; the packing of the basket for Old Martha—and the other basket with the kitten that wilful Soffrona will not leave behind. And this wilfulness is justified—it brings about the happy ending in which the kitten is returned to its mother. Mrs. Sherwood would not have permitted this to happen in her tales of 1818; but she is indulgent to Soffrona, and the assumption seems to be that the little girl will grow out of her spoilt ways.

The woodcuts, which might be the work of Orlando Jewitt, are perfectly in keeping with the tale. The prim little girls in large floppy sun-bonnets sedately reading their penny books under a tree (page 9) are an amusing contrast to the bedraggled pair of the frontispiece, knee-deep in the water as they reach for the kitten. The basket 'to bring home any treasures which they might find' sits on the bank under the foxgloves; a fallen tree leans across the shallow brook just as the author described it. The illustrator obviously enjoyed his task.

In ten years, Mrs. Sherwood's vision of the child's

world had undergone radical change. The children them-selves had not perhaps altered very much: Soffrona and Sophia resemble Lucy and Emily Fairchild and come from a similar home. But the world around them is more spacious and far happier. No memory of old murder haunts this wood, no wicked brothers. The bad little boys are fright-ened and defeated; orphan child and stolen kitten alike have found a home. Soffrona's inattention to the sewing does not hold up the work of charity, although her pertness to the servant brings gentle rebuke. In ten years, Mrs. Sherwood had moved from the world of Dr. Watts to that of Mrs. Ewing.*

* This change in the mood of her writing, from the Evangelical to the relaxed, can be seen in small compass in yet another chapbook, *The Two Dolls*, which draws upon her Indian experiences. Here the book begins in the spirit of an out and out missionary tract (with a moral element that owes something perhaps to Maria Edgeworth) and concludes in unalloyed childish pleasure.

7

Mrs. Sherwood and the Firm of Hatchard

Mrs. Sherwood's second Evangelical publisher was John Hatchard of Piccadilly. With his publication of *The History of the Fairchild Family* in 1818, her writing assumed a new dignity and importance.

John Hatchard (1769–1849), printer of *The Christian Observer*, whole-hearted supporter of Evangelical policy, and highly regarded by Wilberforce and other leaders of the group, was the chief bookseller and publisher for the Clapham Evangelicals. His shop was their biggest outlet for pamphlets and speeches upon such matters of joint religious and political concern as Sunday Observance, Indian missions, and the abolition of slavery; he printed and stocked the annual reports of the many societies founded and supported by enthusiastic Evangelicals, and was himself a member of nineteen, vice-president of one, and a committee member of two.

Widely known too as a Church publishing house and patronized by many clergymen, his Piccadilly bookshop catered likewise to the worldly and the famous. Among its customers were Hannah More, Charles and Fanny Kemble, the Countess of Blessington, the Duke of Wellington, and Queen Charlotte (who, like George III, favoured the cause of the reform of the nation's morals). Nor was Hatchard's stock restricted to the religious and political: the poetry of Cowper and Crabbe, and the English classics from Shakespeare to Dr. Johnson were represented; parents and teachers seeking books for children which blended morality or religion with instruction could select from a variety including *The Parent's Assistant*; the works of Mrs. Trimmer; by 1818, *The History of the Fairchild Family*; and, after 1833, *The Peep of Day*. Among the dozens of tracts stocked were those of Hannah More, Legh Richmond, and the whole selection printed by F. Houlston and Son.

Scrupulously avoiding the sensational, the trivial, and

the ephemeral, John Hatchard cherished the reputation of his business for dignity and decency. Thus his publication of *The History of the Fairchild Family* guaranteed the moral tone of the book as well as bestowing a very real social distinction upon the writer. Upon Mrs. Sherwood's latest offering rested the semi-official approval of Clapham; her theory of education stood henceforth an excellent chance of reaching into the nurseries of upper- and middle-class homes whose owners were socially powerful. Those wealthy businessmen, gentry, Members of Parliament and adherents of the Established Church who formed a large proportion of Hatchard's customers were the actual rulers of the country.

Judging by the number of Mrs. Sherwood's books found today with the elaborate book-plates of former owners, she was very successful in reaching this class of reader. When, for example, Admiral Lord Radstock (a patron of eighteen Evangelical Societies, including the Society for the Suppression of Vice, and the President of the Naval Charitable Society) wished to give a little girl a present, he selected a book from Hatchard's.

Although Hatchard published only ten of Mrs. Sherwood's books, these included *The History of the Fairchild Family* and *The History of Henry Milner* (seven volumes in all). Produced over a period of thirty years, they display Mrs. Sherwood's own fluctuating beliefs, and show the decline of the old Evangelical spirit and the shaping of the Victorian frame of mind. Increasing prosperity, strengthening class consciousness and a deepening of religious rifts are in simplified form all discernible in these seven volumes. The servants John and Betty of Part I of *The History of the Fairchild Family*, who are almost part of the family, are pushed aside in Part III by their gossiping, flattering counterparts in the fine manor-house; the chastened young clergyman does not take to the mission field by the end of *John Marten*: he receives a comfortable living from an aristocratic benefactor.

During this period of rapid social change, a prosperous urban middle class, composed largely of merchants and industrialists, was fast moving upwards and pushing into the ranks of the landed gentry. Within a few years political power would shift from the landowner to the businessman.

Presentation inscription in *Eighteen Maxims of Neatness and Order* by Theresa Tidy, 1818. The donor, Lord Radstock, was one of the most energetic of early nineteenth-century Evangelicals.

Frontispiece to Hatchard's edition of *The Fairchild Family*, 4th ed., London, 1819. (G1.1)

Mrs. Sherwood, like most of her contemporaries, unaware of the long-range political implications of her period, recognized a change in pace in social life and was distressed by increasing secularism and religious and political turmoil. The reforms of 1830, for example, called forth her protests against those who:

... despising all those who had gone before them, and all the wholesome rules and customs of their forefathers, are for establishing a new order of things, and making new experiments, on subjects not only decided in ages past by the wisdom of man, but by the indisputable Word of the Almighty.

(*Emancipation*, 1829, p. 148)

But in 1818, she was still a devout Evangelical, fully convinced that the nation, if not the whole world, had come to a spiritual turning-point. To the specifically Christian (but not always Evangelical) education of the children of the influential upper classes, she devoted her major efforts in the next twenty years.

The publication of the first part of *The History of the Fairchild Family* turned the Evangelical penetration of the nursery that began in 1814 with *The History of Little Henry and his Bearer* into a prolonged occupation. Mrs. Sherwood had shown by her revision of *The Governess* that the ideas of her predecessors could be evangelized, and had demonstrated—in print, at least—the application of Evangelical doctrine in the school. With *The History of the Fairchild Family*, she invaded the family circle. Bringing vital religion back from the remote Indian bungalow or the army barracks, she laid the Evangelical crusade squarely upon the domestic doorstep.

She started *The History of the Fairchild Family* in India on the journey from Cawnpore to Meerut in November 1812, and completed it in its first form a year later. To her flock of children (consisting at that date of her own Lucy and Emily, her orphan girls, Mary Parsons and Sally Pownal, and an unspecified number of other regimental orphans) she read and told the stories that became a staple of Victorian Sunday reading.

'More of *The Child's Manual* written,' she recorded in January 1813, and again:

. . . In the evening we had prayers together, and as I was then writing *The Fairchild Family*, I used on these occasions to read a story out of it and then to use the prayer and hymn.

(*Life and Times* . . ., p. 393)

In May she wrote the story of Mrs. Cutshorter (later 'Mrs. Howard'); in August, 'The Story of the Besetting Sin', completing the book in October. During the same year she had produced *The Ayah and Lady* and the *Stories Explanatory of the Church Catechism*.

Subtitled *The Child's Manual, The History of the Fairchild Family* could equally well be taken as a guide by uncertain parents brought up in a laxer age. In 1818, the 'serious' had become the fashionable; a sort of snob appeal thus commended the book to rising middle-class families to whom it must have seemed an impeccable guide. Obviously respectable, well-educated and pious (though not, in Part I, well-to-do), the Fairchilds lead a life of sober rectitude in their restricted but genteel circumstances. Carefully planned frugality enables them to support a village school and to assist their poor neighbours. Both Mr. and Mrs. Fairchild teach in the Sunday School; even the children have their own little pupils whom they accompany into church. The whole family, including the servants, is meticulous in Sabbath observance. The excellent relationship between master and servant depicted here soon became a casualty of the thrusting Victorian period, but E. M. Forster's account of the Thorntons' household in *Marianne Thornton* attests that it had existed in real life.

Nothing ostentatious or vulgar mars the sober restraint of life in the Fairchild family. Mrs. Sherwood evidently intended the Fairchilds to represent the *type* of the ideal Evangelical family, and as such it was generally accepted for some years. There was, on the surface, no sharp break with the past: adults brought up on the eighteenth-century moral tale recognized the familiar pattern. But moral tales, recast by Mrs. Sherwood, sounded a deeper note, in this case, vital religion in the home, clearly explained, brought to bear upon every situation, every action, every thought.

Many sides of child life at home and abroad are shown: dress and conduct; manners and morals; education and amusement. The little Fairchilds, obedient, industrious, frugal, are brought up in the best eighteenth-century tradition of simplicity. They polish the furniture, keep their clothes in order, help in the garden, sew for the poor, visit the sick. Social relationships in eighteenth-century fashion maintain a perfect balance as the children visit the ailing Charles Trueman on the one hand and Miss Augusta Noble on the other; the subsequent deaths of these two provide object lessons on the necessity of preparation for death. The obituary tract comes vividly to life in the death of Charles Trueman, complete with death-bed, last words, and the funeral. Just as Berquin had inculcated a general morality in his little plays, Mrs. Sherwood inculcated a very particular religion in dramatic narrative interspersed with instruction. Instead of illustrating the consequences of folly (or of what would be called today 'anti-social conduct'), she stressed the consequences of sin, expounding its spiritual dangers in gripping detail.

She was very explicit about sin. Part I of *The History of the Fairchild Family* is dominated by the Evangelical certainty that there are no *little* sins, evil being absolute and without gradation. Since humanity is essentially depraved, every human action is subject to examination in the light of the gospel under which all stand equally convicted of evil. In Evangelical belief, the eye of God sees the covetous thought as one with the actual theft; on the authority of the New Testament, to call one's brother a fool is to rank with Cain. For Mr. Fairchild, the nursery quarrel that led to the notorious interview with his children at the gibbet's foot which Harvey Darton quotes at length in his *Children's Books in England*, was neither trivial nor temporary. It was a serious rift in the cosmic order, which, disregarded, could widen into hatred, unreconciled family quarrels being related *in kind* to war and murder. Any break, no matter how small, in the divinely appointed institutions of family or society is an offence against divine law.

Ever since the seventeenth century, pious works for children had *said* these things, but none had *shown* them so vividly or linked the great spiritual issues so closely with domestic life. Everyday events at nursery level assumed new importance when, in every moral decision, God supported one side and Satan cheered for the other.

Although all episodes in which the little Fairchilds are naughty have serious religious significance, some are particularly emblematic. Names, sometimes reminiscent of eighteenth-century type characters ('Trueman', 'Goodwill', or 'Friendly'), also show the book to be in the line of direct descent from *Everyman* and *The Pilgrim's Progress*. Henry Fairchild, stealing the forbidden apple and compounding his crime with a lie, re-enacts the Fall of Man. Poor Miss Augusta Noble, dying of burns, has (if little readers cared to pursue the parallel) perished literally in the same fashion that she might perish spiritually (as implied by her vanity, disobedience, and untruthfulness and by Mr. Fairchild's conversation with the clergyman after the funeral).

Mr. Fairchild, it appears, was educated for the Church: hence his preoccupation with doctrines and his lengthy expositions of Bible truths. These, with long passages and texts from the Bible, interpolated hymns drawn from Watts, Doddridge, Cowper, and others, and the religious lessons implicit or explicit in the tales, made *The History of the Fairchild Family* an ideal book for Sunday reading. No work for children to date had so thoroughly subordinated instruction and amusement to religion.

The book has aroused both high praise and bitter criticism, being attacked on two main points, both fundamental to Evangelical belief. Its emphasis on human depravity ('wicked hearts', to young readers) conflicts sharply with the romantic Wordsworthian view of innocent childhood and with the sentimental mid-century picture fostered by Dickens's *Old Curiosity Shop* and *Oliver Twist*. Its insistence upon preparation for death, accepted by Victorian readers, is sharply condemned in the present century. Readers of its own time were less troubled by these points; most accepted or genuinely enjoyed the book. Enough recalled it with affection to demand new printings until 1913, and it was still on the lists of the Presbyterian Sunday School offerings in Canada in 1900.

What did children of 1820 find in *The History of the Fairchild Family*? Benjamin Gregory, a Methodist minister, who must have been among the early readers of the book, wrote warmly of its 'unforced humour and its wholesome tenderness'. Lord Frederick Hamilton, a child of the mid-century, recalled that:

There was plenty about eating and drinking; one could always skip the prayers, and there were three or four very brightly written accounts of funerals in it.*

They identified two qualities in the story that modern critics, eyes fixed on Mr. Fairchild and the gibbet, have ignored. The book has the vitality and texture of real life; its remarkably naughty children, whom Mrs. E. M. Field, in *The Child and his Book*, wrote of as 'personal friends', were refreshingly different from the perfect beings of most early Victorian books. All young readers recognized from their own experience the actions and feelings of the little Fairchilds, the childish anger, jealousy, greed and fear that are so vividly evoked. Emily's new doll arouses Lucy's envy, Miss Augusta Noble's coloured sashes, embroidered muslins, and numerous toys leave both little girls dissatisfied with their own quiet nursery. Henry Fairchild, usually better behaved than his sisters, joins in plaguing the servant, and takes down the swing from which, during their careless play, Emily is hurled to lose her two front teeth.

Charlotte Yonge, who owed more to Mrs. Sherwood than she liked to admit, remarks in her article on Didactic Fiction upon the author's 'felicitous descriptions' in *The History of the Fairchild Family*, and 'the gusto with which she dwells on new dolls and little tea-drinkings with good old ladies', as well as on 'the absolutely sensational naughtiness of Henry, Lucy and Emily, and the dreadful punishments they underwent'.*

Dreadful or not, these punishments are related to a second point often overlooked. The little Fairchilds were neither left to the care of servants nor handed over to the outside agencies of school, camp, or cinema. They had at all times their parents' undivided attention. Mr. and Mrs. Fairchild, though strict, are not unpredictable; they explain the reasons for prohibitions and punishments; they invite questions; they are loving and demonstrative.

* Benjamin Gregory is quoted by Richard Altick in *The English Common Reader* (1957), p. 118; Lord Frederick by Marion Lochhead in *Their First Ten Years* (1956), p. 51.
* 'Didactic Fiction' is one of three articles published in *Macmillan's Magazine*, Vol. XX (July, August, September 1869); reprinted in *Signal*, nos. 2–4 (Stroud, 1970–1).

. . . So saying, Mr. Fairchild taught his children a prayer: after which he kissed them, and sent them to play in the garden . . .

Most episodes end thus. Kissed and reassured, tucked into bed by a mother who always had time for them, the little Fairchilds felt thoroughly secure.

The whole matter of 'dreadful punishments' and wicked hearts was not necessarily as frightening as some would have us believe. These are not the young Rudyard Kipling, bewildered, heartsick, and alone in the House of Desolation; they are the cherished offspring of a home in which all the inmates, parents, servants, children, accept the tenets and live by the rules. In one instance the hell-fire theology is hurled at a child made to feel that he alone is threatened; in the other, similar language, quietly uttered, and applied to all, loses most of its force through familiarity. Explanations are given if necessary, and beliefs taken for granted lose half their terror. The Evangelical might have been quite certain that Hell was there; but he knew with equal certainty that he was bound for Heaven. The quality and intellectual content of explanation or belief is not on trial here; the method of its giving is what counts with the young.

Theology apart, Mr. Fairchild is no Mr. Brocklehurst in *Jane Eyre*, and his children welcome his company. Mrs. Fairchild, in guiding Lucy to a better frame of mind, confesses her own tendency to jealousy and envy, her own difficulty in controlling them; then 'Mrs. Fairchild and Lucy knelt down and confessed before God the exceeding vileness of their hearts'. Nor does Mrs. Fairchild force the confidence of her children, who come voluntarily to admit their mischief and tell her their troubles.

In the setting of its own time, *The History of the Fairchild Family* was realistic rather than terrifying. The gibbet in the lonely wood could still have been seen in 1818 and for the next fourteen years; any child out nutting might have stumbled upon it. Moreover it did not invade the family sitting-room as the appalling horrors of this decade can do at the turn of a knob. Sudden death was very common at a time when no germ theory existed to explain outbreaks of fever or plague that were increasing in number and virulence with the congestion of growing slums in industrial cities. Tuberculosis (the 'decline' or 'waste') that carried off whole fictional families, did the same in real life, where the sufferers were nursed devotedly and died at home under conditions guaranteed to pass on their complaint.

Probably wisely under these circumstances, the Evangelicals advocated a deliberate preparation calculated to remove the fear of death by making it familiar and natural. Mr. Fairchild's approach to the subject is matter-of-fact:

'Should you like to see the corpse, my dears?' asked Mr. Fairchild. 'You never saw a corpse, I think?'

'No, Papa,' answered Lucy: 'we should like to see one.'

'You must see these things one time or another,' [Mr. Fairchild concludes] 'and attend dying people: it is therefore better in early life to become acquainted with such things.'

His attitude would have been commended by John Wesley, who approved of the boys at his school, Kingswood, making such a visit. There was another point of view to be considered too: that of etiquette. Betsy Wynne Freemantle, an exact contemporary of Mrs. Sherwood and of the same social class, noted in her Journal in 1804:

Lady Buckingham proposed at breakfast our going to see the corpse of their Under Butler, a young man of 21, who died of consumption . . . the sight was unpleasant and *offensive* to the nose . . . (*The Wynne Diaries*. Ed. Anne Freemantle, 1953. Entry for 6 July 1804)

Evidently such visits were given and received as a mark of respect and sympathy in Georgian times, although growing class distinctions and increasing concern for hygiene put an end to them later.

In 1822, *The History of the Fairchild Family* being an acknowledged success, John Hatchard requested a sequel. He received instead, the first volume of *The History of Henry Milner*. Mrs. Sherwood, incurably subjective in her attitude to her writing, was not then concerned with children of five, six, or seven: her own Lucy, Emily, and Henry were now thirteen, eleven, and nine respectively, and she was thinking ahead. *The History of Henry Milner*, extremely popular in the author's lifetime both in England

and in America, is its author's answer to the educational theories of Rousseau which she detested without really grasping how much her own owed to them. Considering the writing of Rousseau and Voltaire the well-spring of infidelity, she set out after 1822 to counteract their influence. She probably had in mind too the deistical Mr. Thomas Day's *Sandford and Merton*; there are parallels between it and *The History of Henry Milner*.

Her Evangelical and Millenarian Mr. Dalben, the mouthpiece of her own changing religious convictions between 1823 and 1837, is a world apart from Emile's mentor, or Thomas Day's Mr. Barlow. In the latter, all Evangelicals could recognize one of those clergymen of whom the great Joseph Milner (a pioneer of the movement) said that their office was but a secular trade and their lives destitute of religious sensibility. There could be no mistake about the religious basis of Mr. Dalben's educational theories. If, like his creator, he shifted in the course of four volumes and fifteen years from the position of an Evangelical to that of a near-Universalist, he remained aggressively religious. Henry Milner was intended to be a Christian counterpart of an infidel Emile. '. . . not a natural character', Mrs. Sherwood admitted, 'but a renewed and regenerate one'. Rousseau's theory that men are naturally good she denied; where Rousseau emphasized inherent goodness, Mrs. Sherwood exposed original sin:

. . . he knew no naughty words and naughty tricks; notwithstanding which, like all little children, who have not yet received new hearts, he was full of evil inclinations . . . every child born of the family of Adam is utterly corrupt from his birth. . . .
(The History of Henry Milner, Part I, Chapter IV)

Rousseau had deferred moral and spiritual teaching until Emile was sixteen; Mrs. Sherwood, on the contrary, showed it beginning when Henry Milner was three or four. Although exposure to the classical writers was postponed until fourteen on the ground that the mind of childhood is easily tainted by corrupt and pagan ideas, Henry Milner began Latin grammar at nine.

Nevertheless Mrs. Sherwood owed a good deal to Rousseau. Like Emile, Henry Milner grows up in comparative isolation without luxury. Like Emile, too, he lives close to nature at all times, but a nature in which God's shaping hand is forever being pointed out by his mentor:

The book of nature, my dear Henry, is full of holy lessons, ever new and ever varied; and to learn to discover these lessons should be the work of a good education . . .
(*The History of Henry Milner*, Part I, Chapter XVI)

Thus the science that Mr. Barlow makes so much of in *Sandford and Merton* becomes in *The History of Henry Milner* natural history, and lessons invariably end with Mr. Dalben displaying the types and emblems that formed so large a part of Mrs. Sherwood's Millenarian theories.

. . . the promises of future things and of the great mystery of redemption have from the beginning of time been revealed to man under the types and symbols of created things. These types are wholly hidden from the unconverted man . . .
(*The History of Henry Milner*, Part II, Chapter III)

Like the boys in *Sandford and Merton* and the pupils of Madame de Genlis, Henry works in a garden of his own (the garden is a favourite type of the innocent world with Mrs. Sherwood); and he makes things with his hands. Instructing and aiding his own protégé, Maurice O'Grady, he learns the true meaning of charity.

The succeeding volumes of *The History of Henry Milner* came out in 1826, 1831, and 1837, its hero passing in that time through boarding-school and Oxford. The trials that he encountered were mainly spiritual; Mrs. Sherwood depicted vital Christianity in the boarding-school twenty-five years before Thomas Hughes did so. Indeed, like her contemporary, Dr. Arnold (who became head of Rugby in 1828), she could have said 'What I want to see in the school and what I cannot find, is an abhorrence of evil,' and she would have thoroughly approved of his great object of making the school a place of really Christian education.

Mrs. Sherwood marched Henry Milner through Oxford at a pace calculated to keep him exactly in step with young Henry Sherwood, who became curate of White Ladies, Aston, in time to preside at the festivities there for the

Coronation of Queen Victoria. These were exciting years at Oxford—the years of the Catholic Relief Act, of Keble and Pusey, of the Tractarians and the *Tracts for the Times*. She found plenty of cause for alarm, particularly in the Roman Catholic Relief Act of 1829.

Her travels on the Continent in 1831–2 had only confirmed her earlier conviction that Roman Catholicism was both politically dangerous and spiritually akin to classical paganism and to Hinduism. Having a perfect horror of statues and images of any kind, she saw them, not as symbols, but as those 'graven images', specifically condemned in the Bible. Apparently only the works of nature qualified for her system of types and emblems: nothing man-made could be admitted.

An inveterate novel reader and lover of Gothic romance, she fully recognized the romantic appeal of the beauties of Catholic Europe, and was certain that from this quarter emanated the most subtle spiritual danger facing the young in the 1820s. In her view, the rational infidelity of twenty years earlier had now joined hands with an equally evil and infinitely more alluring romantic paganism. Henry Milner was pressed into service in 1837 to counteract it.

. . . '(T)here is something imposing in these symbols of this mysterious power—something grand in these dark shades and this sombre edifice.'

says John Marten, surveying the hidden Catholic chapel in an inaccessible part of the estate of a local landowner. Henry Milner, well coached by Mr. Dalben during the previous three volumes, is able to correct his friend.

. . . 'It is (humanly speaking) to such imposing figures as these, that the papal power has owed its long and lasting influence over the hearts of unregenerate men, having other means whereby to work upon the feelings of those who have been prepared to be influenced by religious motives; and . . . when I looked just now at the fine temple below, the same idea respecting the effect of imagery upon the eye came to my mind in reference to heathen superstitions. I have no doubt that there was a great deal in the forms and ceremonies of the old idolatries of Greece and Rome, which was very captivating.'

(*The History of Henry Milner*, Part IV, Chapter VII)

For young people of the educated and influential upper and middle classes, Mrs. Sherwood produced a number of anti-Catholic warning tales set in France, Italy, and Switzerland, the countries most popular with the English traveller. She aimed at the social level into which Tractarianism and its corollary, creeping Catholicism, were making serious inroads, often, as she knew, among the younger generations of such strict Evangelical families as the Newmans, the Mannings, and the Wilberforces.

Forgetting for the time being the excellent advice she had received in 1795, when *The Critical Review* had advised her to take her materials from common life (A1), Mrs. Sherwood wrote two melodramatic Gothic novels, *The Nun* and *The Monk of Cimiés*. Neither was printed by Hatchard; and Mrs. Sherwood was later rebuked in *The Christian Observer* for sensationalism. *The Monk*, declared the critic, was:

. . . unfair and unconvincing. The party to be praised is made all that is excellent; and the party to be reprobated all that is wicked; and the sympathy of the reader is gained by artificial colouring, instead of the judgment being guided by sober truth.
(May 1837, p. 307)

When she once more took up the anti-Catholic theme in *The History of John Marten* (1844), she handled it with comparative restraint, devoting enough of the book to a young clergyman's troubles in English country parishes to make its neo-Gothic episodes pass muster. The disapproval of the Evangelicals did her reputation no harm: without difficulty she found sympathetic publishers elsewhere.

William Darton, Thomas Melrose, Knight and Lacey, Seeley and Burnside . . . all, it seemed, were happy to print what they could get. Although John Hatchard and his son Thomas remained strictly selective in their offerings, and Mrs. Sherwood was coming to have rivals in her own field (among them Ann Fraser Tytler and Catherine Sinclair), the firm constantly reprinted its earlier titles. In 1842 and 1847 came the long-delayed sequels to *The History of the Fairchild Family*. Mrs. Sherwood's books for young readers of the upper classes were still welcome, for outwardly at least, she conformed in these to Evangelical requirements.

A characteristic wood-engraving done by W. H. Lizars for Thomas Melrose: the frontispiece to *Obedience*, 1830. (F5)

74

Sabbath observance was covered for young readers in *The Little Momiére*, a tale in which, as in *The Flowers of the Forest*, the Evangelical child converts her elders. *Victoria* shows the neglected child being enticed into Catholic beliefs. Nevertheless, Mrs. Sherwood was fast moving out of the Evangelical orbit. In spite of their acceptable doctrine, the religious effect of these books was weakened by narrative and romance: background and landscape with its own intrinsic interest; journeys in France, Switzerland, Italy; conflict not always spiritual. She had long overflowed the limitations to which she had formerly assented; by 1840 the literary climate had moderated and the great age of the Victorian novel was beginning. Having for twenty years made narrative acceptable in the nursery and schoolroom, she must be held partly responsible for this change; her tales had formed the taste, and their moral and religious content had given such writing approved purpose. Can it be only coincidence that Charlotte and Emily Brontë, George Eliot, and Charles Kingsley were all children of Evangelical families who must have known Mrs. Sherwood's tales well?

Her own writing in her later years indicates that she welcomed the change in literary outlook, her religious views having so far softened that she wrote in 1837:

... this same anticipation of evil is no Christian exercise; on the contrary, the Christian is required to rejoice evermore in the full assurance that all that is is right. . . . It is, then, a Christian's duty to enjoy the present, as far as is consistent with moderation, and to trust the future to Him 'by whom all things were created . . .'
(*The History of Henry Milner*, Part IV, Chapter II)

The second volume of *The History of the Fairchild Family* was printed after a lapse of twenty-four years. The reader picks up the story where it left off in 1818, finding the children on the surface much the same, but the tone of the book different. The originals of Lucy and Emily were both dead. Accepting her grief with a resignation that she had not been able to muster twenty-five years earlier, Mrs. Sherwood wrote again of these beloved daughters of her Indian years with tenderness and understanding and far less strict religious doctrine.

Thus Mr. Fairchild, on one of his infrequent appearances, is depicted showing his children the beauty of a flower and the wing of a beetle under the magnifying glass instead of displaying a corpse; he concludes with a prayer for spiritual light, without a word of wicked hearts. He has inherited an estate and a social position; the family standard of living has risen, reflecting no doubt that of the Sherwoods as well as that of the nation as a whole over the period. Mrs. Fairchild still shows to advantage, especially in her sympathetic treatment of the slovenly Bessie, a new character who supplies a good deal of comic relief.

The first and most successful volume of *The History of the Fairchild Family* Mrs. Sherwood left alone. She had 'corrected' it between 1818 and 1822, making a few minor changes which pinpoint accurately the beginnings of the Victorian concern for seriousness and respectability. She began with names.

The hospitable Old Mrs. Cutshorter (her name perhaps coming to be considered frivolous or vulgar) became Old Mrs. Howard. Mrs. Goodwill, for less obvious reasons, became Mrs. Goodriche. Is this an attempt to eliminate a name suggestive of tracts for the lower classes? Did Mr. Hatchard suggest that in the Evangelical circles he knew so well riches and goodness were almost synonymous? We shall never know.

Respectability, too, demanded changes in 'Mrs. Fairchild's Story'. She, who had in her unregenerate childhood 'sat upon the coachman's knee' at midnight feasts in the kitchen with the servants, sat for the rest of the century upon the housemaid's knee. She was not deprived of her titbits of 'toasted cheese and bread sopped in beer'. (Mrs. Sherwood knew that children needed a nourishing diet, and in her books, as in her household, provided it.) Billy, the stable boy, who tempts youthful Mrs. Fairchild to steal cherries, is replaced by 1822 with Nanny, an idle village child. Whereas in the 1818 edition, the little Fairchilds found themselves 'quite drunk' after sampling the farm wife's cider, in 1822 and ever after, they were 'quite tipsy'.

In all this, Mrs. Sherwood altered nothing essential to her main thesis. She would have been distressed by the sweeping changes made later in the century, culminating

pag 209.

Traurige Folgen des Ungehorsams

(BM)

Lithograph by W. Severin for a German edition: *Die Familie Fairschild*. Düsselthal, 1838. (G1.4)

77

An Edwardian view of *The Fairchild Family*. Illustration by Evelyn Beale for the edition of 1908. (G1.14)

A modern illustrator glances at *The Fairchild Family*. Edward Ardizzone's line drawing for the extract in *Naughty Children*. (G1.18)

in the edition of 1902 and those which followed. In these, all Mr. Fairchild's home sermons, all prayers and hymns had vanished. 'Evil thoughts', 'sinful hearts', 'wickedness', and 'general (or universal) depravity' had either disappeared altogether or faded into 'naughtiness'. The significant episodes depending on these terms were deleted or severely curtailed. 'Man Before the Fall' became 'The Birthday Walk', losing its original ending and purpose; and twenty-five episodes shrank to fourteen.

Mrs. Sherwood's Evangelical doctrine was not the only casualty. Her point that parents as well as children must struggle with their own sinful hearts was lost in Victorian revisions where the parent assumed disproportionate importance. As the religious framework was weakened or removed, the parent became the ultimate authority, and the Victorian cult of the family was reinforced in a way that Mrs. Sherwood had never intended.

It must not, however, be forgotten that the 1818 edition was also reprinted near the end of the century; in some quarters the strict Evangelical version was still approved.

Apart from this, material about death had almost disappeared in the revised versions; gone were the visit to the corpse; the gibbet scene; the death of Charles Trueman. Miss Augusta Noble was still burnt to death, but without detail, without funeral, and without speculation on the fate of her soul. Fireproof fabric still being a thing of the future, she became an object lesson of the folly of approaching the open fire in a gauze dress.

Part 2, less stiffly Evangelical than its predecessor, was less severely pruned. 'The Story of Evelyn' in Chapters XXIII and XXIV lost much of its death scene and funeral. Prayers and hymns were everywhere deleted, and Bible verses omitted: in common with Part 1, references which end with the phrase 'For the sake of the Lord Jesus Christ' were removed, presumably because they inculcated too great familiarity with the name of Our Lord. The Victorians, unlike their fathers or grandfathers, the Evangelicals, preferred to keep at a respectful distance from Divinity.

Thus the work which its author had intended as a cornerstone of religious education was thoroughly secularized. No longer was every moment of decision a combat in the Holy War, watched by God and Satan; Good and Evil became Right and Wrong. Few genuine moral decisions remained to be made, for when sin dwindled into naughtiness, an offended God was replaced by a vexed Papa or a hurt Mama.

8

Mrs. Sherwood and the Firm of Darton

Long after she had abandoned Evangelical doctrines, Houlston and Hatchard published new editions of all Mrs. Sherwood's early works and brought out the sequels that she supplied in the 1840s. Most of her new titles after 1830 were published by Darton, a firm established about 1785 by the elder William Darton, a Quaker, remembered chiefly for his association with the Taylors of Ongar. William Darton the younger maintained after 1810 a separate establishment on Holborn Hill, where he published numerous children's books, including 'Peter Parley' volumes both genuine and spurious; work by the Howitts; and many of Mrs. Sherwood's later stories. In 1854, Darton published her autobiography (edited by her daughter, Sophia Kelly); and in 1862, the Journal of Mrs. Cameron with its interesting sidelights on the life of the Sherwoods. The history of this firm has been briefly outlined by F. J. Harvey Darton in *Children's Books in England*; in 1910 he edited *The Life and Times of Mrs. Sherwood*.

William Darton the younger started with a modest number of Mrs. Sherwood's tales, some extracted from *The Youth's Magazine* (H6). Thanks to his habit of printing each tale several times (i.e. singly or two together, and in one or more of the many annuals, keepsakes and collections in which the firm specialized), he rapidly built up the number of his copyrights and compounded the confusion of bibliographers to come (e.g. items H6, H7, and H8). Darton's well-known aversion to dating his offerings undoubtedly arose from this practice; the exasperation of customers in his own day is indicated by the Advertisement to *The Cloak* (1836):

It is but right to state that the following Tales are from the *New Year's Token* of 1835, a useful and instructive Annual; and should the young reader have that Book, any respectable Bookseller, where this was purchased, will, on that account, willingly exchange it for any other publication of similar price.

THE CLOAK

Or wine them in garlands round their hats

Page 19

One of the illustrations around which Mrs. Sherwood wrote a story: frontispiece to *The Cloak*, 1836. (Possibly an engraving by Thomas Fairland from a picture by Robert Farrier.) (H11)

One hopes that the respectable booksellers co-operated.

Darton published Mrs. Sherwood's 'secular' works (i.e. those in which religion is secondary to narrative). Some of these resemble eighteenth-century moral tales; others are largely informative. Many were written at William Darton's request around little woodcuts that he sent to be worked into a story. As might be expected, the result is often a veritable rag-bag of incident and illustration. The shilling books extracted from *The Holiday Keepsake* and *The Juvenile Forget-me-Not* are examples of longer tales produced thus, the best being *Grandmama Parker* . . . into which Mrs. Sherwood packed some lively episodes of her husband's boyhood adventures during the French Revolution. In spite of such absurdities as *Jack the Sailor Boy*, she usually brought to this monotonous task considerable ingenuity; she would never have left (as her daughter, Sophia, did) a black and lumpy rhinoceros gazing morosely out of a totally unrelated story. The occasional failure of a frontispiece to correspond to any tale in the book may be dismissed as the publisher's fault: the economical William Darton (whose stocks of text and illustration never seemed to come out even) often used the same plates in two or more works.

Nevertheless, of all Mrs. Sherwood's publishers, Darton alone took a genuine and imaginative interest in illustration, faithfully investigating each new process as it appeared. Baxter colour printing; stipple engraving on stone; copper and steel engraving; the early work of Harrison Weir and Edmund Evans are all to be found among his offerings, often lending artistic or historic interest to otherwise mediocre work.

Mrs. Sherwood's writing for Darton was not confined to the mechanical production of tales on order. She had found him sympathetic towards fiction and narrative at the moment when she turned back to the novel. Long before her Evangelical enthusiasm had cooled,* Evangelical

* *Religious Fashion, or The History of Anna* (1827) contains a tart argument against young people joining Evangelical societies, 'professing circles', where 'young people are taught to use the language of religion before the spirit of it has touched their hearts, and to make a parade of their Christian virtues, while in fact they have nothing more than the semblance of them.' (*Religious Fashion*, pp. 52, 53). (See Appendix, J12, Am. S.S.U.).

Illustration by Harrison Weir from *Brotherly Love*, London, 1851. (H25)

reviewers were alarmed by her increased drift towards fiction. In 1816, *The Evangelical Magazine* had warned its readers that Mrs. Sherwood's use of narrative in *Stories Explanatory of the Church Catechism* was too diverting. In 1821, the reviewer suggested that she was writing more than 'a just estimate of her mental furniture would dictate'. Unconcerned, she wrote on, justifying herself in the Preface to Volume I of *Roxobel* (1830–1):

The writer is aware that an extended narrative, which, if natural, must embrace various stages and conditions of human life, is rejected by many worthy persons, as not being a desirable mode of conveying instruction: and there can be no question but that this form of composition . . . has often been rendered an exceedingly powerful engine in the hands of the evil one. But, because an engine is powerful, should it, merely on that account, be relinquished to the foe? And if some have been busy in directing this engine against the bulwarks of religion and morality, should others refuse to use it in the case of godliness?

She made no attempt to placate her more vehement critics, of whom the local reviewer of *Emancipation* is probably typical:

. . . her insidious writings, under the guise of friendship, have brought contempt upon religion, and diffused all the evils of novel-reading through numerous families where they could not, otherwise, have been introduced . . .

(*Worcestershire Miscellany*, 1831, pp. 155–7)

Even the widespread anti-Catholic feeling of the 1830s did not make *The Nun* (1833) and *The Monk of Cimiés* acceptable in Evangelical circles. The last was published by William Darton, who was, perhaps, aware of the general change in literary taste that was incubating the great age of the Victorian novel.

Mrs. Sherwood, evidently convinced by this time that:

It is too much the error of religious persons to despise elegant literature and science—the one being valuable from the insight it gives to the work of God in the mind of man, the other to the work of God in the material world. (*The Little Momiére*, p. 40)

86

welcomed the moderation in the literary climate. In her writing after 1835, entertainment takes precedence over religion. A number of pleasant tales, novels, or romances for the young, show her chameleon-like ability to take on other colours, echo a plot, adapt an idea, a character, or a mode of speech to her own purpose. In 1826, *The Gipsy Babes*, her most attractive version of the tragic 'Babes in the Wood', displayed the influence of Scott's *Guy Mannering*: a child is stolen for revenge; an old gipsy woman protects him and restores him to his family. Mrs. Sherwood nevertheless contributed much of her own—limiting the whole tale to three or four years, inventing a charming little gipsy girl, making the gipsy grandmother a moving and memorable figure in her own right, and giving the tale its dream-like atmosphere and happy ending. Nor did she neglect religion, which appears without moralizing in her advocacy of 'that kindness which every Christian owes to a fellow-creature, however degraded'. The picture of the gipsies is a forerunner of the romantic Victorian conception, and far from that approved by the Evangelicals; Mrs. Sherwood laid her emphasis, not like Hannah More, upon dishonesty and dirt, but upon human affections: the old gipsy woman who protects the helpless children has both dignity and worth. She seems to have been the first writer for children to reject the accepted stereotypes of the gipsy as either a sort of nursery ogre-cum-enchanter or a squalid poacher and petty thief. Possibly she was influenced by the current campaign to ameliorate the wretched lot of the gipsy population.* She returned to the theme at least twice afterwards, but not with the same compassion shown in *The Gipsy Babes*.

With the publication of *Shanty the Blacksmith* in 1835, Mrs. Sherwood defied Evangelical scruples against fiction to produce a well-constructed Gothic romance for the young. The book contains most of the elements of the popular novel save romantic love. Like its predecessor *The Gipsy Babes*, it is based upon the traditional fear and suspicion of the gipsy; as in the Gothic novels, the gipsies add colour and romance, and help to carry the plot. *The*

* For a brief discussion of the presence of gipsies and Jews in nineteenth-century children's books, see the first note at the end of this chapter.

He went to Shanty's forge.

(The Osborne Collection, Toronto Public Library.)

A stone-engraved frontispiece by J. Marchant to *Shanty the Blacksmith, A Tale of Other Times,* London, c. 1841. (H5)

Gipsy Babes begins with a child being kidnapped by gipsies; *Shanty the Blacksmith* introduces a child abandoned by a gipsy at a lonely forge in the north of England. For the moment, Mrs. Sherwood even admits a faint whisper of the diabolic: the gipsy lad, Harefoot, comes first to the forge to seek a horseshoe because he is 'plagued with one of them witches'. Strictly rebuked by old Shanty, Mrs. Sherwood's mouthpiece and the voice of common sense in this book, Harefoot persists, and within a few minutes the woman who may be the witch herself, enters in a shower of sleet: 'a tall gaunt female, covered with a ragged cloak . . . speaking in a broad northern dialect'. She carries the drugged child, abandoning it in a corner not long after Shanty has looked at it with anxiety, 'unable for some minutes to satisfy himself, or to put away the horrible fear that he might, perchance, be looking at a body without life'.

It is a gripping beginning to an exciting tale. Its Gothic touches came naturally to Mrs. Sherwood, who distributed them generously but not implausibly: lost heir, ruined castle, humble helpers and faithful retainer, sinister and mysterious gipsies, prisoner and plot . . . all the elements are there with the orphan, Tamar, at the heart of the tale. More stories of this sort would have assured her a permanent place in children's literature.

In true romantic style, the gipsy reappears, keeping the suspense high by her cryptic speeches with a double significance that Tamar (now about fifteen) misinterprets:

'Do you mind me?' said the gipsy; 'I have known you long—aye, very long. You were very small when I brought you to this place. I did well for you then. Are you grateful?'

Tamar now did turn and look at her, and look eagerly and carefully, and intently on her dark and weather-beaten countenance.

'Ah!' said the gipsy, whilst a smile of scorn distorted her lip, 'so you will demean yourself now to look upon me; and you would like to know what I could tell you?'

'Indeed, indeed I would!' exclaimed Tamar, all flushed and trembling. 'Oh! in pity, in mercy, tell me who I am and who are my parents?—if they still live; if I have any chance or hope of seeing them?'

'One is no more,' replied the gipsy. 'She from whom I took you lies in the earth on Norwood Common. I stretched the corpse myself; it was a bonny corpse.'

Tamar fetched a deep, a very deep sigh. 'Does my father live?' she asked.

'Your father!' repeated the gipsy, with a malignant laugh—'your father!'

Tamar became more and more agitated; but excessive feeling made her appear almost insensible. With great effort she repeated, 'Does my father live?'

'He does,' replied the woman with a malignant smile, 'and shall I tell you where and how?—shut up, confined in a stronghold, caught like a vile animal in a trap. Do you understand me, Tamar? I think they call you Tamar.'

'What!' said the poor girl, gasping for breath, 'is my father a convicted felon?'

'I used no such words,' replied the gipsy; 'but I told you he lies shut up: and he is watched and guarded too, I tell you.'

Following the conventions of the Gothic novel, Mrs. Sherwood makes the gipsy woman contribute to clearing up the mystery and establishing Tamar as the child of the wealthy Jew, Mr. Salmon. By 1835, the popular novel had accepted the Jew as a romantic figure (Note 1); the Millenarians were committed to a form of Zionism; and Mrs. Sherwood, always involved in Old Testament studies and the emblematic significance of the Hebrew language, was able to combine romance and religion with considerable success. Evangelical doctrine is kept to a minimum; there are touches of humour; and the eccentric laird and his elderly aunt—good-hearted but not religious—are treated with affectionate tolerance.

Mrs. Sherwood did not look only to Scott and the Gothic writers for a model. *Intimate Friends* and *Caroline Mordaunt* show a lively, humorous, and satirical strain. Caroline's encounters with her various employers, her conversations with her disillusioned elderly guardian, and the characterization of Miss Kitty in *Intimate Friends* parallel similar episodes in the work of Jane Austen or Jane Taylor, and may well have been inspired by these two writers. The ironic resignation of Caroline's old cousin as his sprightly young relative is handed back to him time after time by her

(BM)

Engraved frontispiece to *Intimate Friends*, 2nd ed., 1834. (C32)

various employers is almost on a par with Mr. Bennet's remarks about his younger daughters. Miss Kitty is a younger version of vulgar Lucy Steele of *Sense and Sensibility*; she chatters like Lydia Bennet and has Isabella Thorpe's taste in novels (her malapropisms being italicized):

I have got Charlotte and *Walter* worked in chenelles for my grandmother, which was done at school, and *Peter* weeping over *Flora's* tomb, to answer to it, and a filagree caddy, and a doll dressed in the latest fashion, in a balloon hat and all, and several very nice books, there is 'The Sorrows of Sensibility', and 'The Tears of the Heart', and 'The Weeping Hero', and 'The Rose of the Desert', and several more . . .

Like her probable prototypes in *Northanger Abbey* or *Sense and Sensibility*, Miss Kitty does no permanent harm. After she involves the narrator, Belle, in a series of deceptions in which both girls are finally exposed and humiliated, silly Belle is at last convinced that:

. . . brothers and sisters are friends and companions appointed by the Almighty; and that, in most cases, they are fast friends, who . . . cannot choose but to be interested in each other's welfare. . . . Hence, the advice of a brother or of a sister may always be welcomed as being more pure and disinterested than that of strangers . . .

The lesson may be the same as that of earlier books, but the gay, lively style has a strong flavour of that levity forbidden to the Evangelical. As in *Caroline Mordaunt*, the proportion of didactic and overtly religious material has shrunk to make room for comic action and realistic dialogue.

There is, on the whole, a good deal in the tales published by Darton which supports the reviewer's complaint that Mrs. Sherwood had helped to usher in an age of novel reading. She had fostered the taste for narrative and made the tale (as distinct from the tract) respectable, colourful, and highly emotional.

Many of her later tales were written in partnership with her youngest daughter, Sophia.* One result was a number

* For a summary of the complications of Sophia Sherwood as author, see the second note at the end of this chapter.

of historical romances: *The Mirror of Maidens*, *The Two Knights*, and *The De Cliffords*. Although Charlotte Yonge (a Tractarian) complained that in the last book 'The poor Shepherd—Lord Clifford is brought in as an advanced Calvinist', this aspect of the tale is less obvious than its watery sentimentality, a mark of almost everything in which Sophia had a guiding hand. She was probably responsible, too, for the increased preoccupation with class with which Mrs. Sherwood in her earlier books was not much concerned. Class distinction in her generation and background was natural; taken for granted, it rarely intruded; 'neither were the times such as rendered the affectionate intercourse between different ranks in society, almost, if not altogether, impracticable, as it now would be', she wrote with regret in later years (*Life and Times*, p. 202).

A note on the nineteenth-century literary interest in gipsies and Jews

In addition to numerous folk-tales and ballads about gipsies, much material was available in print during Mrs. Sherwood's lifetime. Hannah More's Cheap Repository Tracts, Ser. I (Nos. 442, 443), *Black Giles the Poacher*, and *Tawney Rachel, or The Fortune-Teller*, both written as warnings to ignorant country folk against the wiles of such vagrants, were still in print in 1860. Their warnings were repeated for children by William Darton the elder: *Little Truths for the Instruction of Children* (London, 1802); and in *Rural Scenes, or A Peep into the Country* (London, 1806), illustrated and revised by Ann and Jane Taylor.

On the other hand, a genuine concern with the welfare of the much-persecuted gipsies was shown by the Quaker reformer, John Hoyland, who produced in 1816 the first well-documented factual study of the British gipsies: *A Historical Survey of the Customs, Habits, and Present State of the Gipsies*, designed to promote the Amelioration of their Condition (York, 1816). The Methodist preacher, James Crabb (1774–1851), 'took an active interest in the welfare of the gipsies of the New Forest' (*D.N.B.*), and wrote a tract entitled 'The Gipsies' Advocate' on their behalf; a volume dedicated to James Crabb, 'the Gipsies' Friend', is advertised by Hatchard in 1844. The well-known Anglican missionary to Red River, John West, on his return from Canada opened a school and a mission for the gipsies at Chettle in Dorsetshire.

Sir Walter Scott's novels, *Guy Mannering* (1815) and *The Heart of Midlothian* (1818), with their dramatic and sympathetic presentation of the gipsies, were augmented by his articles in *Blackwood's Edinburgh Magazine* (beginning April 1817). Mrs. Sherwood was not the only children's writer to follow his romantic treatment of the gipsies; in 1838, Jane Strickland produced *Lady Mary and her Gipsey Maid* (London, Dean and Munday).

In similar fashion, the Jew became a sympathetic figure in romantic and Victorian literature about this time. Scott again seems to have been partly responsible: Rebecca and Isaac of York greatly influenced later writers. Grace Aguilar became a popular writer with the young; and Old Testament studies (perhaps as a counterbalance to Tractarianism) flourished. There was a Society for the Conversion of the Jews; and a Presbyterian Mission of Enquiry to the Jews was sent out in 1839 to travel over Europe and the Middle East.

A note on the work of Sophia Sherwood

The names which accompany Mrs. Sherwood's on the title-pages of books published in the 1840s are, at different times, 'Streeten Butt', 'Mrs. Streeten', 'Mrs. Kelly'. All three represent the same person: Mrs. Sherwood's youngest daughter, Sophia, who began writing about 1833 as 'Miss S. Sherwood'.

Thomas Melrose published *The Rosary* . . . (1833); and *The Drooping Lily* (1835). The first of these went into *The Garland* in 1835 (and subsequently into Harper's *Works*, Vol. 14) as Mrs. Sherwood's, and Sophia never retrieved it. With Houlston she published *The Scarlet Lobelia* (listed around 1840 by the publisher); and *The Fortescue Family* (listed 1849 as by Mrs. Streeten).

In 1833, Emily Sherwood Streeten died, and Sophia subsequently married her brother-in-law, Dr. R. J. Nicol Streeten. As 'Streeten Butt' she appeared as co-author of *The De Cliffords* in the first printing, afterwards as Mrs. Streeten. In 1849, Dr. Streeten died, and two years later,

Mrs. Sherwood. Within a year or two of her mother's death, Sophia married Dr. Hubert Kelly, writing thenceforth as Mrs. Kelly.

A list of her better-known works appears in the B.M. Catalogue under Streeten; several of the books she wrote with Mrs. Sherwood are listed with the latter. She edited her mother's Autobiography (1854) in true Victorian fashion; but in spite of suppressions and almost total omission of dates, it contains some details omitted by Darton. Her style is sentimental and often gushing, far inferior to her mother's. In 1871 she edited *Susannah, or the Three Guardians*, and apparently *The History of Little Henry and his Bearer*, for the Book Society's reprints. (See also notes to Items H20, 22, 25, 27; and the whole set of items H29 etc.)

9

Mrs. Sherwood and Later Generations

By 1851, the year of Mrs. Sherwood's death, the children of the Evangelical ascendency had grown into the early Victorian reformers. Counterparts in real life of the little Fairchilds, of Henry Milner, Little William, Little Robert, and Soffrona, they were heirs to the indestructible eighteenth-century moral tradition with its emphasis on benevolence, as well as to the equally durable, highly-concentrated Evangelical education that insisted upon vital religion, moral decision, and doing the next thing.

No less religious than their parents, they had significantly shifted the premisses of belief. Many, in fact, rejecting their early Evangelicalism, turned to Liberal Christianity, to Tractarianism, to Roman Catholicism, or to free-thinking. Could they, the regenerated children of a world that had so recently established a rigid standard of respectability, be expected to acknowledge the universal depravity of mankind in general and their own wicked hearts in particular? The 'manners of the nation' had improved beyond all recognition. Whatever its actual spiritual state, by 1850, the nation complied outwardly to a greatly elevated moral standard; took missionary work for granted and paid for it; and hotly discouraged slavery anywhere in the world. As energetic and decisive as their parents, the Victorians sought and found their own causes: factory reforms, the health of towns, and the rehabilitation of the slum-dwellers were among them. They had a profound faith in education; unlike the Evangelicals, who had seen ignorance as a lack of spiritual understanding, the Victorians saw it as a lack of practical knowledge as well, knowledge essential to human progress in the complex material world of the mid-century.

As control of education shifted by degrees from the churches to the state, books for children became more secular—save for Sunday reading and books for the newly-literate. Printed by the tract societies, the latter were strongly religious in tone, direct literary descendants of

Mrs. Sherwood's earlier Evangelical tales, which retained an honoured place among them. Her later tales were read mainly by upper- and middle-class readers. She was thus, as Charlotte Yonge pointed out in her 1869 article on 'Didactic Fiction':

. . . the mother of two genera of books—the religious story of the poor and of the rich . . .

The third type of her literary offspring was perhaps the most influential of all—the missionary story.

These stories, which in themselves kept alive the missionary spirit and perpetuated that paternal attitude towards India that lasted into the present century, were widely imitated. An unfortunate assumption of racial superiority was fostered by the over-simplification of some of Mrs. Sherwood's successors; by 1850, the old Evangelical fervour had evaporated, leaving a residue that she had never intended. The idea of the Christian child converting the old pagan, strong in sentiment and religious appeal, induced likewise an unbecoming national vanity.

Mrs. Sherwood and most of the earlier Evangelicals may be absolved of this trait. An uncompromising belief in the universal depravity of the human heart saved them: for they did not flinch from applying it to themselves.

'Then,' said the Ayah, 'Ma'am must keep the copra for herself, for she alone is good, . . . she is without fault.'

'Ayah,' said the Lady, 'you know now that you are saying what is not true; . . . every day I do wrong things: how often have you seen me angry without reason, and idle when I ought to be serving God, and proud and fretful. I do not pretend to be good, Ayah. I know I never was, nor ever shall be truly good. . . . I do not consider myself without fault, but as a very great and miserable sinner. . . .' (*The Ayah and Lady*, 13th ed., p. 15)

Later writers of missionary tales, however, such as Charlotte Tucker (A.L.O.E.) preferred to stress instead the evils of Indian religions, 'the degrading thraldom in which millions of our fellow-creatures, our fellow-subjects, are held by Satan, the father of lies', pointing out the happiness of 'a land bathed in the light of Christianity . . . where children are taught almost from the cradle the value of honesty and truth'.*

Mrs. Sherwood's school stories, too, had elements of the missionary tale; long before Thomas Hughes wrote *Tom Brown's Schooldays*, she had introduced serious religious decisions into the school story (formerly the preserve of the moralist).

Her contribution to the association between religious belief and family life has already been discussed. The Victorians adopted it with enthusiasm after suitable qualification. By 1843, for instance, it was felt in some quarters that Mrs. Sherwood's insistence upon the parent's acknowledgement of his own wicked heart was superfluous and disruptive: Miss Rigby complained in the *Quarterly Review* of:

. . . her manifold pictures of weak and wicked parents—bad schools—despicable governesses—and detestable clergymen—to say nothing of the irreverence with which she treats all that is high in social position, and the suspicion she attaches to whatever is respectable in external appearance . . .

(Vol. LXXII, 1843, Article II)

The omniscient Victorian parent was not the creation of Mrs. Sherwood, but of the Victorians themselves; nevertheless, by presenting the parent as God's vicar in the family, she had planted and fostered the idea. Closely allied to it was the high value placed on innocence, for she saw little value in experience. True, the romantic picture of childhood innocence did not tally with the theme of universal depravity that she had disseminated during her Evangelical period, but she reached a reconcilation in her later works. *The History of Henry Milner*, Part IV, for instance, sets forth the principle that:

. . . those to whom the Divine spirit is imparted . . . in very early youth, before the natural corruptions have been brought into exercise and strengthened by action . . . are above nature.

* A.L.O.E.: Prefaces to *Little Bullets from Batala* (*c*. 1880) and *A Wreath of Indian Stories* (n.d., *c*. 1880). A.L.O.E. had no compunction about ignoring the findings of the London City Mission.

Henry Milner himself and a number of her schoolgirl heroines such as Anna (who is found in *Juliana Oakley* and *Ermina*) and Sophia (*The Broken Hyacinth*) represent such ideally innocent youth.

Other themes restated by Mrs. Sherwood, and literary forms adapted by her for children's books, continued in use for the rest of the century. Victorian writers of allegory, seeing in it a means of offsetting the growing materialism of the times, followed Mrs. Sherwood closely. Charles Kingsley in 1848 asserts the theory of types as applied to the family relationship:

... through these family ties, and by those family names ... God reveals Himself to man, and reveals man's relations to Him ... else why has God used those relations as symbols of the highest mysteries ... ?

(Charles Kingsley, *His Letters and Memories of his Life*, 1883, p. 76)

Mrs. Gatty's *Parables from Nature*, although it displays a superior knowledge of science, arrives at conclusions only a step in advance of Mrs. Sherwood's. Bishop Wilberforce's *Agathos* has obvious parallels with *The Infant's Progress*. In the general secularization of children's books during the century, the allegory of Mrs. Sherwood and Mrs. Cameron was followed by tales such as *The King of the Golden River*, *The Water Babies*, or *The Princess and the Goblin*.

Much of Victorian historical fiction for children—the books of Emma Leslie, for instance, or Mrs. Charles—turning upon religious battles of the past, took the narrowly Protestant view for which Mrs. Sherwood's anti-Catholic writings of the 1830s had prepared the ground. Charlotte Yonge, critical of Mrs. Sherwood's religious teachings, conceded that her writing had 'a simplicity and earnestness of detail that go to the very heart's core'; a modern reader feels that *The Heir of Redclyffe* is also to some extent the heir of *Henry Milner* (an outgrowth, perhaps, as Tractarianism was an outgrowth of Evangelicalism).

By the end of the century, the works of Mrs. Sherwood might have been out of sight for six days a week in many nurseries, but their basic principles were never entirely out of mind. Whether they were recognizable as hers or not is immaterial: they had become part of the very foundation of middle-class family life. Sunday reading—the Victorian compromise with the Evangelical insistence that all children's literature be religious or instructive—was likely to include one or more of *The History of the Fairchild Family*, *The Little Woodman and his Dog Caesar*, *Stories Explanatory of the Church Catechism*, or *The Infant's Progress*. In Sunday schools, *The History of Little Henry and his Bearer* (or *The History of Lucy and her Dhaye*) still illustrated the continuing need for foreign missions; and some of Mrs. Sherwood's penny or twopenny chapbooks were issued as 'rewards'. Above all, there was the comforting assurance of an ordered world (for serious cracks in its structure were not widely apparent until after 1914); and of an ordered family life in which parental authority still had the sanction of religion.

THE LITTLE WOODMAN
and his Dog Caesar

❦

SOFFRONA
and her Cat Muff

Facsimile Reproductions

FRONTISPIECE.

Little William in his Grandmother's Cottage.

THE

LITTLE WOODMAN,

AND HIS

DOG CÆSAR.

BY MRS. SHERWOOD,

Author of "Little Henry and his Bearer," &c. &c.

TWELFTH EDITION.

Wellington, Salop:

PRINTED BY AND FOR F. HOULSTON AND SON.
And sold at their Warehouse, 65, Paternoster-Row,
London.

1828.

[Entered at Stationers' Hall.]

[Blank]

THE

LITTLE WOODMAN,

&c.

———❦———

IN former times there lived, on the borders of a very wide forest, a certain wood-cutter, named Roger Hardfoot, who had seven sons. I cannot tell you the names of the six elder sons; but the youngest, who was born several years after his brothers, was called William.

A 3

The wood-cutter's wife died when William was very little : so the care of the boys was left to their father only. He was an industrious man, and gained a very good livelihood by cutting wood in the forest, and tying it up in faggots. These he conveyed, on the backs of asses, to a small town at some distance; and with the money which he sold them for, he brought back such things as he had need of for himself and his family.

He made his sons also work with him; and, as they were

hearty lads, the elder ones soon became able to do almost as much as their father: so that the earnings of the family were very abundant, and they might have been very happy, had not that one thing been wanting without which no family can be happy. The wood-cutter was so sinful as to neglect to teach his children to serve God: and this was the more wicked, as he had himself been taught the word of God by his mother when he was a little boy.

But the wood-cutter neither

thought of his Saviour nor of his poor mother's instructions, until God brought him to reflection by a dreadful accident. One day, while he and his sons were cutting down a tree in the forest, the tree fell upon him, and he was so dreadfully hurt, that he never was able to work any more. His hurt occasioned a disease which, by slow degrees, brought on his death. But while death was drawing on, he suffered great pain of body, and his mind was filled with many bitter thoughts: all the sins of his past life were set before him by the almighty power of God; particularly his neglect of his mother, who was a widow, and from whom he had run away many years ago. And now he began to remind his sons of their duty to God; frequently speaking to them of their Saviour, and of the world to come.

From day to day the poor dying woodman earnestly besought his sons to turn to God; but they mocked at him, and would not hearken to him. He could now work for them no longer, nor provide them with what they wanted: so they followed their own business and pleasure, hardly taking care to furnish their sick father with common food or clothing. One only of all his sons took pity on him, and hearkened to his advice, and waited upon him. This was little William, his youngest child. He was just five years old at the time when the tree fell upon his father, and his heart was not yet grown hard, like the hearts of his brothers.

Fathers and mothers, you should lead your children to love

God while they are little, and while their hearts are tender. And you, little children, lose no time, but give yourselves up to God before you become hard and stubborn, like William's brothers.

William was now the only comfort his poor father had in this world. When the wood-cutter lay sick upon his bed, William sat on his bolster, and watched beside him, and was always ready to bring him every thing that he wanted. And when his father crept out into the forest, which he sometimes was able to do in order to take the air, William followed him ; and when he sat down, this little boy sat by him ; and when he knelt to pray, little William knelt by him, and prayed with him as well as he could.

One day, when the woodman's eldest sons were gone out to steal deer in the forest, the woodman and his little boy sat at the door of their hut ; while Cæsar, little William's dog, lay down at their feet. And as they sat together the woodman thus talked to his little boy :—

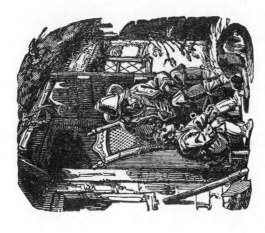

The Wood-cutter talking to his Son William at the Door of his Hut.

B

"Oh! my little child! my only comfort!" he said, "how wicked was I when your young like you, that I did not endeavour to lead them to God! But that opportunity is past, and I can do nothing for them now. They will not hearken to me; they turn against their dying father; and I deserve this treatment at their hands."

"Why do you say that you deserve it, father?" said William.

"For many reasons, my dear

[Blank]

boy. I was an undutiful son; and for this cause, if there were no other, I deserve to have undutiful children. My mother was a widow, and one who loved God. Her house is in this forest; but three or four long days' journey from this place. I was her only child. She brought me up, with the greatest tenderness, and taught me early the word of God. But when I grew up I became a lover of pleasure more than a lover of God; so I ran away from my dear mother, and have never seen or heard of her since."

"And is she alive?" said little William.

"Oh! my child, I do not know," said the wood-cutter; "but whether she be alive or dead, I shall never see her again in this world. I only wish that she could know how deeply I repent of my sins; and that I have fled at length to the merits of a gracious Redeemer, as my only hope of being saved from everlasting punishment. And O, my sons! my sons! I pray for my sons in the bitterness of my soul: for as I was formerly a wicked son, so I have since been a wicked father. I neglected to teach my children the word of God while they were little; and now they despise me, turning a deaf ear to my instructions, and hardening their hearts against my reproofs!"

"But," said William, "perhaps the Lord Jesus Christ may change their hearts even now, father. Let us pray for them."

"Yes, my child! my comfort! my delight!" said the woodcutter, "we will pray for them. Every day while I live we will

pray for them. This is all I can now do for them."

So William and his father knelt together at the door of the hut, earnestly praying that God would, in his good time, change the hearts of the young men.

The wood-cutter did not live long after this discourse had passed between himself and his little son. In a few days he took to his bed, from which he never rose again. William now became more attentive to him than ever; and never left him but to fetch him water, and such things as he asked for. William sat on his bolster, and Cæsar lay at his feet; and whenever the wood-man was heard to lift up his voice in prayer, his little boy prayed with him.

On the morning of the day on which he died, he told his little boy that he trusted his prayers had been heard, and that his sins were forgiven him for his Savi-our's sake. He then prayed ear-nestly for his elder sons; after which, kissing little William seve-ral times, he besought him to

Little William joining his dying Father
in Prayer.

remember his Saviour in the days of his youth.

Towards evening, William's brothers came in with a deer which they had killed in the forest, and a cask of brandy which they had bought from some travellers; when making a great fire in the hut, they roasted part of the venison, and opened their cask of brandy. They took no notice of their poor dying father, though they could not help knowing the state he was in. However, they invited William to come and feast with

[Blank]

them; but this kind little boy would not leave his father. He sat beside him till he grew very drowsy, and then laying himself down by him on his bed, he fell asleep.

In the morning, when he awoke, he found his father quite dead, and his brothers lying asleep in different parts of the hut. So kissing his poor father, he sat crying by him till his brothers awoke.

But, not to make this story too long, I must tell you, that

the young men buried their father, the day after his death, in a dark corner of the forest, not far from the hut. And when they had closed up the grave, and covered it with sod, they returned to the hut, leaving William and Cæsar sitting by the grave.

After returning to the hut, the young men sat down to regale themselves with the remainder of the venison and the brandy. And they began to plot mischief against their little brother, whom they sorely hated, be-

cause his ways were not like
their ways. "We must not keep
him with us," said one of them,
"lest, when we kill the king's
deer, he should tell of our
practices."

"But we will not kill him,"
said another, "lest his blood
should rise up against us."

"Let us take him three days'
journey into the forest," said a
third, "and there suddenly leave
him. He will then never come
back to tell tales of his brethren."

"But we must take care to
tie up Cæsar in the hut," said a
fourth, "or we shall find him
very troublesome. There will be
no getting him away from the
child."

"To-morrow," said the fifth
brother, "we will set out. We
will take an ass with us to carry
the child; and we will go three
long days' journey into the depths
of the forest."

"But we must carefully con-
ceal our purpose from the child,"
said the sixth, "that we may

not be troubled with his lamentations."

So these wicked young men having settled their horrible plan, they got up early the next morning, and, preparing one of the strongest of their asses, they took their little brother out of his bed, and, hastily helping him to dress, set him upon the ass.

"Where are we going?" said William, who thought no evil.

"We are going," answered the

[Blank]

elder brother, "three days' journey to hunt in the forest, and you are to go with us."

"What! hunt the king's deer?" said William.

His brothers made no answer, but looked at each other.

Cæsar was ready to follow the ass on which his little master rode, wagging his tail, and capering about, to shew that he was in a hurry to be gone; but one of the brothers came with a cord, which he fastened round

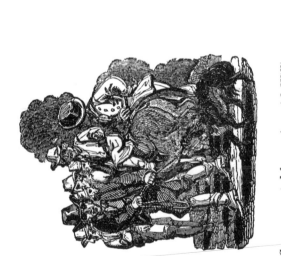

Cæsar prevented from going with William.

the poor dog's neck, and dragged him into the hut.

"May not Cæsar go with us?" said William.

"No," said the elder brother.

"But we shall be away several days; will you not leave him something to eat?" added William.

"Mind your own business, child," answered the brother: "we will take care of Cæsar."

So Cæsar was tied up in the hut; and all the brothers being now ready, they gave the ass a stroke with a stick, and began their journey into the forest.

They first went down a deep, dark path, where the trees were so thick that the light of heaven was almost shut out: then they began to ascend a steep hill, sometimes turning to the right, and sometimes to the left. Thus they went on as fast as the ass could trot, pursuing their journey till noon; when they stopped under a large oak tree to feed the ass, and to take some refreshment themselves, which they had brought in leathern bags upon their backs.

After an hour's rest, they began their journey again, and went on till evening; when they came to a cave, in a deep hollow way, near which a spring of water gushed out of the rock. At the mouth of this cave the brothers lighted a fire, for fear of wild beasts, and having eaten their supper, they laid themselves down to sleep.

The next day they continued their journey into the depths of the forest, where they saw many deer, which peeped at them from among the underwood, and then ran away. At night they slept on a little circle of grass, which they found in an open part of the forest. But one of the brothers was obliged to watch all night, to keep up a large fire, which they had lighted for fear of the wolves, whom they heard all night howling and baying around them.

The next morning they began their last day's journey. The

ass was much tired; but this, however, did not disturb these hard-hearted young men. They drove the poor creature forward without mercy, taking little rest, till they came, towards dusk, to a place where four ways met. Here they halted, and having lighted a fire, they sat down to eat and drink.

"We have been travelling three days," said little William; "are we now at our journey's end?"

"Do you think we are come far enough?" said the elder brother, laughing.

"I do not know what you are come for, brother," answered William.

"To steal the king's deer," replied the young man.

"But there are deer much nearer our hut than this place; why should you come so far to steal deer?"

"You will know soon enough," was the only answer they returned.

D

So after they had eaten their supper, they all lay down to sleep; every one without saying his prayers, excepting little William, who, though he was much tired, fell upon his knees to pray. He joined his little hands, as he had been taught to do by his poor father, and called upon God, in the name of his Redeemer, to take care of him. "My father is dead," said he to himself, "and my brothers speak roughly to me. I have no friend in this world to care for me. O my God! do thou take care of me, for my dear Saviour's sake,"

When he had finished this prayer, he lay down by the ass, and was falling asleep, when he fancied he heard these words: "*I will. Be not afraid.*" At this, he raised up his head, and looked about to discover the speaker; but his brothers were all asleep about him, excepting the one who was watching the fire, who sat silently with his elbows upon his knees. Then the little boy thought that these words had been put into his mind by his heavenly Father; so he felt comforted, and lay down again to sleep.

Now little William was very much tired, and he slept so soundly, that he never heard his brothers move: for these wicked young men, in pursuance of their horrible scheme, got up before break of day, and, leading away the ass, silently departed towards their own house, leaving William in a deep sleep upon the grass.

William continued to sleep, being undisturbed, till the sun was high enough to shine hot upon him through the upper parts of the trees. Two daws chattering in a branch above his head now awakened him; when he sat up, and looked round him. The turf on which he had been sleeping was interspersed with many beautiful flowers; there was the violet, the wood anemone, and the many-coloured vetch; and birds of various kinds were hopping about, singing and chirping among the trees. It was a lovely morning; and the leaves of the trees were scarcely moved by the gentle wind.

William at first could not recollect where he was, or how he came into that place. But when he perceived that his companions were gone, and that he was left quite alone, he began to cry bitterly, and to call out aloud for his brothers. His voice sounded through the wood, but no answer was returned. His brethren were already many miles distant from him.

"Oh! my brothers! my cruel brothers!" said William, "did you bring me here in order to leave me in this place? Oh! my father! my poor father! could you now see your little boy, how grieved you would be! But you are happy. I hope you are with God. Yet though you cannot see me, God can see me; and he will pity me, and take care of me. If the wild beasts should eat my body, my soul will go to heaven. My Saviour will pity me. I am a little sinful boy; but my Saviour came to die for sinners."

Then little William did what all children should do in trouble; he knelt down and prayed for God's help, and he prayed very earnestly.

Little William praying in the Wood.

After he had done praying, he thought that he would try to follow his brothers: but then he recollected, that, as four ways met in that place, it would be impossible for him to know which way they went. He looked to see if there were any marks of fresh footsteps in any of the roads, but could not find any. He then returned to the place where he had slept, and, sitting down on the grass, began to weep bitterly. But he never allowed a word of complaint to proceed out of his lips: only from time to time he prayed

earnestly for help from Heaven; and his prayers were always made in the name of his Saviour.

Sometimes it came into his mind that his brothers were only gone a-hunting, and that they would come back again in the evening; and this made him unwilling to leave the place in which they had left him.

Towards mid-day, being very hungry and thirsty, he began to look carefully about for any bits or scraps of bread and meat which his brothers might have left on the grass. He found some, which he ate thankfully; and in searching among the bushes he met with a little spring of water, of which he drank and was refreshed.

Thus God provided him with a meal in the wilderness, where no man dwelt. So poor little William was very thankful, and his trust in God was made greater by this kindness.

My dear little children, when God sends you smaller blessings, be thankful for them. God loves

a thankful disposition. It is a sign of a humble mind; and God loves a humble mind; for it is written in the Bible, *God resisteth the proud, but he giveth grace to the humble.*

And now the time of William's hardest trial came on; but his heavenly Father remembered him, and had provided a place of comfort for him. But you shall hear how it was.

As evening approached, the wood became more and more gloomy. The birds ceased to sing, and went to rest upon the boughs of the trees; the crickets chirped among the dry leaves; and great bats began to flit about, flapping their heavy wings among the branches above his head. Poor little William began now to think how he should spend the night, and where he could be safe from the wild beasts; for he had given up all hopes of his brothers' return. He looked about for a tree into which he might climb, for he was not able to get into a very high one, being but a little boy. After some time he met with one, which he

contrived to ascend, and among the branches of which he endeavoured to fix himself firmly. But he feared that he could not keep himself awake all night; though he did not dare to go to sleep, lest he should fall down from the tree.

Soon after this it became very dark, and the wind arose and whistled dismally through the woods. But what was still worse than the wind, he heard the distant howling of a wolf, which made his little heart to beat; so he sat trembling from head to foot. His fear, however, had the right effect: it did not make him cry; but it urged him to pray. He prayed that his heavenly Father would be with him in his trouble; and his prayer was made, as before, in the name of that Saviour, to whom his father, the poor woodman, had for the last few months of his life, taken so much pains to lead his young heart.

The tree into which William had climbed was directly facing one of the four ways I before spoke of; and while he was praying, suddenly he perceived a light, as of a candle or fire,

which seemed to be at the end of this way or path. This was a sign that some person was near, who, perhaps, might take pity upon him. He did not wait a moment, but lifting up his heart in thankfulness to God, he came hastily down from the tree, and ran towards the place where he had seen the light. But being upon the ground, he could see the light no longer; nevertheless, remembering the direction in which it had appeared, he ran that way with all his might; for he was in great fear of wolves, with which the forest abounded.

The path he had taken went over very uneven ground, leading him sometimes up hill, and sometimes down. So when he had gone on for about half a mile, and had reached a favourable ascent, he saw the light again, which looked nearer and brighter than before. This comforted him greatly; and though he did not stop running, he lifted up his heart in thankfulness to Heaven. He lost sight of the light, however, almost immediately, the path just then leading him down into a deep valley or bottom.

As he was running down into this valley, some clouds rolled away, and he saw the moon. It was not the full moon, but the new moon, which looked like a beautiful silver crescent rising above the woods. By its cheering light he could perceive that a stream of water ran across the bottom of the valley; and this filled him with fear, not knowing how deep or wide the water might be, nor how he should get across it. But he still kept running on towards it, till his little feet began to ache sadly.

breath; and presently he felt the tongue of the animal, put out, as he thought, to begin to devour him. But instead of biting or hurting him, the creature began to lick him, and to utter a cry of joy, by which William knew him to be his faithful dog Cæsar, who had broke the rope that bound him at home, and had come all the way through the forest in search of his little master.

O! how delighted was the little boy when he found that, instead of an enemy, it was his

And here he had a most dreadful fright—for as he was running on, he heard feet padding after him, like the feet of some wild beast, and a panting, which he supposed to be that of a wolf. It came nearer and nearer, till at length poor little William was so terrified that he could run no longer, but fell down at his full length upon the ground, believing that the next moment he should be torn to pieces. And now the creature came close up to him, putting his head so near to William's cheek, that the affrighted child could perceive his only earthly friend! his dear Cæsar! He soon got up from the ground, and hugged Cæsar round the neck; while the poor dog capered about, and played all manner of tricks, to shew his joy.

At last, little William remembered that he was still in the wood, in a place of great danger; so he began to run forward again, and went on as fast as he could, till he came to the water I before mentioned. There he was quite at a stand, not knowing how deep the water

might be; but hearing the howling of a wolf not very far distant, he stepped into the water, and tried to make his way through it. But the stream suddenly bore him off his feet; and he certainly would have been drowned, had not his faithful Cæsar dragged him up, and brought him safely to the opposite side.

Little William felt his heart full of gratitude to his faithful dog, and more so to Him who had sent him such a friend. But there was at present no time for delay; he shook the water from himself as well as he could, and then began to climb the further bank, followed closely by Cæsar. And now the clouds rolled over the moon again, and made it quite dark: but still William felt comforted by the presence of such a friend as Cæsar.

So they went on together, and had almost reached the top of the hill, when William saw in the dark, not far before him, two glaring eyes of some dreadful beast; and at the same time he heard a snarling noise like that of a wolf. He stood still, while Cæsar came before him and began, in his turn, to growl angrily. At length William saw the eyes move, and perceived the wild creature to spring upon Cæsar. For a few minutes there was a dreadful noise and a horrible battle between the faithful dog and the wolf; for this creature was, indeed, a wolf, who was lying in wait for prey on the side of the road.

The woods sounded on all sides with the cries of the two furious animals; and little Wil-

Little William and his Dog Cæsar running
away after the Attack of the Wolf.

liam, not willing to leave Cæsar, though unable to assist him, continued on his knees lifting up his hands and eyes to God: for he knew very well, that if the wolf overcame Cæsar, he would next fall upon him.

For a few dreadful minutes William knew not which would be the conqueror. At length the wolf ran howling away; and the next minute Cæsar came up to his master, and pulled him by the coat, as if it were to persuade him to hasten forward.

William then ran on, and Cæsar with him, till they came to the top of the hill; when, O what a pleasant sight! they saw, not a hundred yards before them, a cottage standing in a garden: for the light from the window was so strong, that they could see even the garden-rails, and the little wicket. William set up a shout of joy and thankfulness, and ran down the gentle slope to the gate, which he opened in a minute, and shutting it after himself and Caesar, began to knock at the cottage-door. But so great was his impatience and

[Blank]

fear lest another wolf should come after him, that he knocked three times before an answer could be returned.

At length he heard the voice of a woman within saying, "Who is there?"

William answered, "A poor little boy, who has been lost in the forest, and who would have been killed by a wolf, if his dog had not saved him."

"Come in, then, come in,"

door. "Come in, poor little fellow: you and your dog are both welcome."

When the door was open, little William saw an old woman stooping with age, dressed in a clean blue woollen gown, and having a white cap tied under her chin. And her house was as neat as herself. There was a bright fire on the hearth, the same which had given light to poor William in the forest, before which was standing an armchair, and a little three-legged

upon it. William did not know it was a Bible at that time, but he learnt what it was afterwards. An old grey cat sat purring by the fire. There was a comfortable clean bed in one corner of the room; and there were many shelves, filled with bright pewter dishes against the wall. "Come in, my little wandering boy," said the good old woman; "come in, you are welcome here." So she brought him and Cæsar into her cottage, and fastened the door.

The moment William saw the

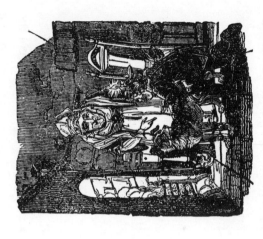

Little William caressing his Dog Cæsar in the old Woman's Cottage.

door shut, and found himself safe from the wolves, he fell down upon his knees, and thanked God for his safe deliverance from death. Then turning to Cæsar, "O! my dear Cæsar," he said, "my dear Cæsar! twice you have saved me from death! If it had not been for you, I should, at this moment, have been eaten up by wolves."

While William was kissing and thanking Cæsar, he perceived a wound in his side, which the wolf had given him, but which

[Blank]

ed till he had brought his lit-tle master out of danger. As soon as William saw the wound he began to cry bitterly, begging the old woman to give him something to cure his poor dog.

"Do not cry, my little boy," said the old woman; "we can do nothing for Cæsar's wound: he will lick it well himself. But I will make him a soft bed by the fire-side, and give him something to eat and drink, and it will shortly get well."

So she brought out an old

sheep's skin, and laying it on one side of the fire, she pointed to Cæsar to lie down upon it. Then going to her pantry, she brought him some bits of meat, and set before him a pan of water. Now the poor dog was very hungry and thirsty, for he had been without food for several days: so he ate and drank; and when he had licked his wound, he fell asleep.

"And now, my little boy," said the old woman, "as you have made your dog easy," (for she could not get the

G

child's attention till Cæsar had been relieved,) "tell me, had you no other friend with you in the forest except this dog?"

"No," said the little boy.

"Well then, my child, endeavour to make yourself easy. To-morrow you shall tell me who you are, and where you come from: but now you shall have something to eat. I must first however wash your poor little weary feet, and dry your clothes; and you shall then go to bed."

Little William could not help crying, when the old woman spoke so kindly to him.

"Why do you cry, my little boy?" said she.

"To think of God's goodness to me," answered William. "A very little while ago I expected to be torn to pieces by wild beasts, and now I am come to you, and am made so happy!"

"Poor little boy!" said the

you happy, you shall be happy."
And she kissed his little wet
cheek.

Then she put some milk upon
the fire, with bread broke into
it; and while it was warming
she took off William's wet
clothes, and having washed the
dust and mire from him, she
wrapped him in a blanket, and
laid him in her bed, hanging his
clothes to dry against the morning: after which she brought
him the warm milk and bread,
and fed him with her own
hands.

The old Woman putting William to Bed.

G 3

"I cannot go to sleep till I have thanked God," said William, "and till I have kissed you, for you are as kind to me as my dear father was."

"And have you not a father now?" said the old woman.

"No," said William, "for he is dead. I have six brothers, but they don't love me: and, after my father died, they brought me three days' journey into the forest; and last night, when I was asleep, they left me to be eaten by the wolves. But

[Blank]

God had pity on me. He brought me to you; and now I will be your child, and love you as I did my father."

"And you shall be my child," said the old woman. "I will love you; and we will serve God together, for you ought to love God very much, seeing what he has done for you."

"My father taught me to love God before he died," answered William, "but he could not persuade my brothers to hearken to

him, when he would have taught them about God."

Then little William told the old woman many things which had passed before his father's death; and how his father had talked to him about his former life, and had repented of his sins, and died trusting in his Redeemer.

While William spoke, the old woman trembled, and was obliged to sit down on the bed by which she was standing; for she began to have some suspicion that William's father was her own son, who had run away from her many years ago, and of whom she had never since received any tidings. For some minutes she could not speak. At length, she said, "Tell me what was your father's name."

"Roger Hardfoot," answered William.

"Oh!" said the old woman, putting her hands together, "it is even so——Roger Hardfoot was my son! my only son! And did he die repenting of

his sins, and trusting in his Saviour? Then my prayers have been heard for him. And are you his child? are you my own little grandson? Were you sent by kind Providence to take shelter in your poor old grandmother's house, and to be the comfort of her old age?" Then she fell upon his neck, and they both wept for joy.

"Indeed, indeed," said little William when he could speak, "this is a wonderful day! And we will thank God together. And did my brothers bring me so far that I might find my grandmother? I shall now love Cæsar more than ever, for I never should have come here, if Cæsar had not helped me through the water, and fought that dreadful wolf."

Now little William was very much tired, and soon fell asleep; but his grandmother (whose full heart would scarcely allow her to close her eyes) spent most of the night in praise and thanksgiving. She thanked God that her son, who had caused her so many hours of sorrow, had

died in faith; and that her little grandchild had been brought to her in so wonderful a manner. Moreover, she prayed that God would turn the hearts of her elder grandchildren, those wicked young men who had used their little brother so cruelly.

William continued to live with his grandmother till he grew up to be a man, and he did everything in his power to make her happy. He took care of her goats, and her fowls, and worked in her garden; and she taught

H

him to read his Bible, and to write. They took great care of Cæsar as long as he lived, and when he died William buried him in the garden.

William lived very happily with his grandmother, because she brought him up in the fear of God; and while he was little she punished him when he was naughty.

She often used to say, " I loved your father so foolishly that I never corrected him, so God corrected me. But I will

love you, my little grandson, with a wiser love, and will not fail to punish you when you are naughty."

When William grew up he thanked his grandmother for having preserved him from doing wrong. And thus their days were spent happily in diligent labour; while their evenings were closed with reading God's book and praying together; till, at length, the pious old woman died.

At her death, she left William

her house, and all that she had; and he mourned for her many months. At length, finding it melancholy to live alone, he chose himself a wife, who feared God; and God blessed him with several children, whom he brought up in the way of holiness.

When William was forty years old, or more, he was sitting at his door one fine evening in summer, with his wife and children about him, and his youngest daughter was reading a chapter from the old Bible which had belonged to his grandmother,

[Blank]

when six very miserable looking men came from the way of the forest. They were pale, and seemed to be worn with disease and famine. On their shoulders they carried old leathern bags, which seemed to have nothing in them. They had neither shoes nor stockings; and their ragged and tattered garments hardly hung upon their backs. They came up and stood before the paling of William's garden, and humbly asked for a morsel of bread.

"We are poor miserable men."

Six poor Men imploring William's Charity.

they said, "and have been many days without any other food than such wild nuts and fruits as we could pick up in the forest; and for several nights past we have had no rest, through our fear of the wolves."

"I ought to pity you," said William, "for when I was a little boy I passed a whole day, and part of a night, alone in that forest, and should have been eaten up by one of those dreadful creatures, had not my faithful dog, whose grave is in this garden, fought for me, and saved me."

While William spoke, the men looked at each other.

"But you seem weary and hungry," said William; "sit down on the grass, and we will quickly bring you something to eat."

So William's wife ran into the house, and prepared a large mess of broth, into which she broke some brown bread, and gave it to one of her sons to set before the men.

The poor half-starved and ragged strangers received the broth with thankfulness, and ate it greedily; after which, they a-rose, and, bowing low before William, they asked him, if he would allow them to lodge for that night with his goats. "For," said they, "we have had no place of safety to repose in for many nights, and are so spent and worn out with watching against the wolves, that we are like men at the point of death."

"I have," said William, "a little barn, in which I keep hay for my goats; you are welcome

to sleep in it, and we will sup-ply you with blankets to cover you. So sit down, and be at ease."

The men were exceedingly thankful; and William opening his gate to them, they came into his garden, and sitting down round him upon the green turf, he entered into discourse with them, while his wife and chil-dren went about their work.

"And whence," said William, "do you come? and where do you propose to go to-morrow?

You seem to have made a long journey, and to be in a very forlorn condition; some of you also appear to be in bad health, and look like men who have suffered much."

"Sir," answered one of the men, who seemed to be the eldest, "we were woodmen, living in the forest, about three days' journey from this place; but some years ago falling under the displeasure of the king, our hut was burnt, all our things were taken from us, and we ourselves were cast into prison, where we lay many years in a lonesome dungeon, so that our health was utterly destroyed; and when we were set at liberty we were unable to work, and, having no friends, we have wandered ever since from place to place, suffering all imaginable hardships, and being often many days without food."

"I fear," answered William, "that you committed some crime, by which you offended the king."

"Yes, Sir," answered the oldest of the men, "we were guilty of deer-stealing. We will not deceive you. We would now live honestly, and lead better lives: but in our own neighbourhood no one will look upon us, and we cannot raise money to buy even a single hatchet to cut wood, otherwise we would follow our old trade, and endeavour to maintain ourselves; though indeed we are now so feeble that we could do but little."

"But," said William, whose

poor men, and to be drawn strongly towards them, "have you no relations in your own country? Are you all of one family?"

"We have no other relations," answered the old man; "but we are all brothers—children of the same parents. Our father was a wood-cutter: his name was Roger Hardfoot."

"And had you not a little brother?" asked William, getting up and coming close to

The men looked at each other like persons in a great terror, and knew not what to answer.

"I am that little brother," said William. "God preserved me from death, and brought me to this house, where I found my grandmother still living, and a parent she was indeed to me; and here I have lived in peace and abundance ever since. Be not afraid, my brothers; I freely forgive you, as God, I hope, will forgive me. You have done me no harm; and now Providence has brought you hither, I will assist and comfort you. You shall suffer want no more."

William's brethren could not answer him,—but they fell at his feet, shedding tears of repentance; for God had touched their hearts in their prison, and had made them sensible of the great and horrible sinfulness of their lives.

William tried to raise them, but they would not be lifted up till they had received his pardon. "We never have prospered since we left you, our little brother, in the wood," they said. "Our lives have, from that day, been filled with trouble, though they were for years afterwards spent in riot, confusion, and sin."

William, at length, persuaded them to rise, and to feel assured that he freely forgave them, earnestly begging them to apply to God for forgiveness through his beloved Son.

The poor men were comforted by William's kindness; but whenever they looked at him and re-

membered how they had treated him, they were filled again and again with shame and sorrow.

The next day William and his sons began to build a hut close by his own cottage for his brothers; and his brothers gave all the assistance in their power to the work.

When the hut was finished, William provided them with mattresses to sleep on, and sheepskins to cover them. He gave each of them a knife, a spoon, a wooden stool, a pewter plate and a horn drinking-cup. He gave them, also, a deal table, and several other little articles of household-goods; while wife and daughters supplied them with coarse clothing of their own spinning.

William was so kind also as to bestow upon each of them a hatchet, which enabled them to maintain themselves by wood-cutting without being a heavy burden on their brother, although he constantly supplied them with many little comforts from his own house.

But what was better than supplying their bodily wants, he took unwearied pains to lead their souls to God. He read to them every evening out of their grandmother's Bible; and it is believed that they did not hear the word of God read in vain: for they became very humble, daily lamenting their sins, and died at last in hopes of being forgiven for their Saviour's sake.

William and his wife lived many years after the death of his six elder brothers, and had the pleasure of seeing their children's children growing up in the fear of God.

And now, my dear children, I would have you learn from this story to make God your friend : *for such as be blessed of him shall inherit the earth; while they that be cursed of him shall be cut off.* (Psalm xxxvii. 22.)

FINIS.

[Blank]

SOFFRONA

AND HER

CAT MUFF.

By Mrs. Sherwood,

Author of "Little Henry and his Bearer," &c. &c.

WELLINGTON, SALOP:

PRINTED BY AND FOR HOULSTON AND SON.

And sold at their Warehouse, 65, Paternoster-
Row, London.

Price Two-pence.

[Entered at Stationers' Hall.]

[Blank]

SOFFRONA

AND HER

CAT MUFF.

BY MRS. SHERWOOD,

Author of

"LITTLE HENRY & HIS BEARER,"

&c. &c.

Wellington, Salop:

PRINTED BY AND FOR HOULSTON AND SON.

And sold at their Warehouse, 65, Paternoster-Row, London.

1828.

[Entered at Stationers' Hall.]

FRONTISPIECE.

See Page 11.

SOFFRONA

AND HER

CAT MUFF.

◆

LITTLE Soffrona lived with a lady who loved her very much. She was not the lady's own child, but she was as dear to that lady as if she had been so, and the child always called her mamma. The lady had a little girl of her own called Sophia. Sophia was one year older than Soffrona; and Sophia and Soffrona learned lessons together, and played together, and were very happy in each

[Blank]

other's company. When you saw Soffrona, you might be sure Sophia was not very far off; and when you saw Sophia, it was very certain that Soffrona was at no great distance.

How delightful it is for little children to live in love and peace one with another! Hear what David says on this subject—*Behold, how good and pleasant it is for brethren to dwell together in unity!* (Psalm cxxxiii. 1.)

Soffrona and Sophia lived in a very lovely house, surrounded with woods. Wherever you looked from the windows of that house, you might see trees growing thickly together, forming beautiful arbours, and pleasant shades, with little paths

winding about among those trees; and here and there, near the trees, were fountains of water springing from the hills, and running down into the valleys: for there were hills there, and the tops of some of them were covered all through the winter with snow, though in summer they appeared green or blue, according to the time of the year, and wore a very pleasant aspect.

Soffrona and Sophia were allowed to play in these woods, and they had learned to run and skip upon the hills like young fawns. It was very pleasing to see them, and they found many treasures in those wild places which children who have never been in woods have no idea of. They found snail-shells, and painting-stones, and wild strawberries, and bilberries, and walnuts, and hazel nuts, and beautiful moss, and many kinds of flowers; and there they heard birds sing—cuckoos, and linnets, and blackbirds, and thrushes; and saw beautiful butterflies with gold and purple plumes, and dragon-flies, whose wings look like fine silk net.

One morning in the month of May, Soffrona and Sophia had leave given to them to play in the woods, after they had finished their lessons, and they took a basket with them, to bring home any treasures which they might find. And they went a long way through the woods,—I dare say as much as half a mile,—till they came

to a place where an old tree had been blown down by the side of a brook; and there they sat down, and each of them took a little penny book to read out of their basket: and while they were reading, they heard a noise of boys shouting and laughing, and they jumped up and hid themselves behind some bushes.

So the boys came nearer, and went
down close to the water's side; and
the little girls heard them say one to
another, " Let us put it in the deep-
est place, where it cannot scramble
out." And they saw the boys stoop
over the water and put something
into it, and at the same time they
heard a very young kitten cry; and
the two little girls could not stop
themselves from screaming out, quite
loud, from the midst of the bushes,
saying, " Wicked, cruel boys! what
are you doing?"

Now the boys heard the cries of
the little girls; and, as the Bible
says, *The wicked flee when no man
pursueth*; (Prov. xxviii. 1.) so they
all took to their heels, and ran away

as fast as they could, leaving the poor
little kitten in the water.

Soffrona and Sophia did not lose
one moment after the boys were gone,
but ran to the brook, and found the
little kitten almost dead. However,
they got it out, though they wet
themselves up to the knees in so doing, and they returned to the tree,
and Soffrona sat down, and laid it
upon her lap, while Sophia wiped
it dry; and as she rubbed it, she
found warmth returning to its little
body, and presently it opened its
eyes and began to mew. " O my
dear little Puss!" said Soffrona,
" how very glad I am that you are
not dead! You shall be my Puss,
and I will call you Muff. Will you

let her be mine, Sophia? Will you give me your share of her?"

Sophia did not say a word against this request, for it was the same to her whether the little kitten was called hers or Soffrona's, and she liked to oblige Soffrona: besides, Sophia was a year older than Soffrona, and it might be expected that she would be more moderate in her desires, and think less of herself. Sophia had lived twelve months longer than Soffrona in the world; and how much may a person learn, with the blessing of God, in twelve months!

So it was agreed that the kitten should belong to Soffrona, and be called Muff; and when the little girls had dried it as well as they could,

they put it into the basket upon some soft moss, and ran home with it.

The lady was not angry with them for having wetted themselves in the brook to save a poor little animal's life, but she hastened to change their clothes; and then they took the kitten out of the basket, and procured some milk to feed it with.

When the fur of the little cat was

quite dry, it was seen that she was very beautifully marked. Her legs, and face, and breast, were quite white, and her back was streaked with yellow and black; so that she appeared like a fine polished tortoise-shell. But she was only nine or ten days old, and was not able to lap milk; and this was a great grief to

Soffrona and Sophia, for they feared that although she had been saved from the water, she would surely die of hunger. The little girls tried to force milk down her throat with a spoon; but the milk ran down the outside of her mouth, instead of the inside of her throat, and the little creature's sides became quite hollow for want of nourishment.

Soffrona was thinking of nothing but Muff all the evening, and she kept her on her lap while she was reading and while she was eating her supper. She was, indeed, so much occupied by her little kitten, that, when the lady asked her to help to make a flannel petticoat for a poor old woman who lived in a cottage among the hills, not very far off, she took the needle in her hand, it is true, but I do not think that she took twenty stitches; for she was looking down every minute upon the kitten on her lap: and the petticoat would not have been done that night, if Sophia had not been doubly diligent.

Now it was much to be wished that the petticoat should be done that night; for it was intended for a good old woman who lived in the woods, a very poor woman indeed, and the March winds had given her great pain in her limbs, and she was in much need of a warm petticoat; and, more than that, the lady had promised the little girls the pleasure of taking the petticoat, with some tea and sugar,

the next morning, after they had re-peated their lessons, to the cottage. But, as I before said, Soffrona's heart was with her kitten, and she could think of nothing else, and of no other creature. She had no pity left for the old woman, so much was she thinking of little Muff. We ought to be kind to animals; but our first affections should be given to our Maker, our second to our fellow-creatures, and our third to any poor animals which may be in our power.

The last thing Soffrona did in the evening, was to try to put some milk down Muff's throat, and this was the first thing she did in the morning: and so far she did right, for the poor little thing depended on her. But

when she had done all she could for
Muff, she should have given her mind
to her other duties; but she could
not command herself to attend to any
thing else all that morning, and learned her lessons so ill, that, if the lady
had not been very indulgent, she would
have deprived her of the pleasure of
walking with Sophia to see the old
woman, and to carry the petticoat.

There was a neat little maid-ser-
vant, called Jane, who used to walk
out with Sophia and Soffrona when
they had a long way to go; and Jane
was ready waiting for the little girls
by the time the lessons were done.

Sophia had asked leave to carry
the basket with the petticoat and the
tea and sugar; and Soffrona took an-

other basket, and put a bit of flannel
at the bottom of it, and laid Muff in
it, and tied the cover over it; and
when Sophia took up her basket to
carry, Soffrona also put her arm
under the handle of Muff's basket,
and went down stairs with it.

When they were got out of the
house, Jane said, "What, have you
two baskets, young ladies, full of
good things, to carry to old Martha?
Well, I am very glad; for she is a
good and pious old woman."

Soffrona coloured, but did not answer; and Sophia smiled, and said,
"She has not got any thing for the
old woman in her basket: she has
only got Muff, wrapped in flannel, in
it."

"O, Miss!" said Jane, "how can you think of doing such a thing? What a trouble it will be to you to carry the kitten all the way! and we have two miles to walk, and most of it up hill. Please to let me carry the kitten back to the house."

"No, no, Jane," said Soffrona, "no, you shall not."

"*Shall* not, Miss!" said Jane: "is that a pretty word?"

Soffrona looked very cross, and Jane was turning back to complain to the lady: but Sophia entreated her not to do it; and Soffrona submitted to ask her pardon for being rude, and promised to behave better, if she would permit her to carry the kitten where she was going. So that

matter was settled, and Jane and the little girls proceeded.

I could tell you much about the pretty places through which they passed in going to poor Martha's cottage, which were quite new to the little girls. They first went through some dark woods, where the trees met over their heads like the

arches in a church; and then they
came to a dingle, where water was
running at the bottom, and they crossed the water by a wooden bridge;
then they had to climb up such a
steep, such a very steep hill, covered with bushes; then they came to
a high field surrounded with trees,
and in a corner of that field was
old Martha's thatched cottage. It
was a poor place: the walls were
black-and-white, and there were two
windows, one of which was in the
thatch, and one below, and a door,
half of which was open; for it was
such a door as you see in cottages,
the lower part of which can be shut
while the other is open. There was
a little smoke coming out of the chim-

ney, for Martha was cooking her po-
tatoes for her dinner.

"Do you think Martha has any
milk in her house?" said Soffrona;
"for poor Muff must be very hungry
by this time."

"I fear not," replied Jane: "but
come, young ladies, we have been a
long time getting up this hill, and we
must be at home by three o'clock."

So they went on, and came close to
the door, and stood there a little
while, looking in. They saw within
the cottage a very small kitchen; but
it was neat, and there was nothing
out of its place. There was a wide
chimney in the kitchen; and in the
chimney a fire of sticks, over which
hung a little kettle. Old Martha

was sitting on a stool within the chimney. She was dressed in a blue petticoat and jacket, and had a high crowned, old-fashioned felt hat on her head, and a coarse clean check handkerchief on her neck. Before her was a spinning-wheel, which she was turning very diligently, for she could not see to do any work besides

spinning; and by the fire, on the hob, sat a fine tortoise-shell cat, which was the old woman's only companion. "O!" cried little Soffrona, "there is a cat! I see a cat!"

"Dear, Miss," said Jane, "you can think of nothing but cats."

"Well, Jane," answered Sophia, "and if she is fond of cats, is there any harm in it?"

Jane could make no answer, for by this time old Martha had seen them, and came halting on her crutch to meet them, and to offer them all the seats in her house; and these were only a three-legged stool and two old chairs.

Sophia then presented the old woman with what she had brought from her mamma, and Jane gave her a bottle of medicine from her pocket: and the old woman spoke of the goodness of Almighty God, who had put it into the lady's heart to provide her with what she needed most in this world.

Now, while Sophia and Jane and Martha were looking over the things which the lady had sent, the old cat had left the hob, and had come to Soffrona, and was staring wildly, and mewing in a strange way round the basket; and at the same time the kitten within began to mew. "Puss! Puss! pretty Puss!" said Soffrona, for she was half afraid of this large cat, and yet at the same time very well inclined to form a friendship with her.

At length, those that were with her in the cottage saw what was passing; and Martha said, "Don't be afraid, Miss; Tibby won't hurt you. Poor thing! she is in great trouble, and has been so ever since yesterday."

"What trouble?" said Soffrona.

"Some rude boys came in yesterday, and stole her kitten," replied

Martha. "I was in the wood, picking a few sticks, and left the door open; and the boys came in, and ran away with the kitten; and the poor cat has been moaning and grieving like a human being,—poor dumb thing,—ever since. The cruel lads! I saw them go down the hill!"

"O!" said Soffrona, "and I do believe"——

"And I am sure," said Sophia.

"And I am so glad!" said Soffrona.

"And how happy she will be!" said Sophia.

And Soffrona immediately set down her basket and opened it, and put the little kitten on the floor, for the kitten was indeed poor Tibby's kitten.

It was a pretty sight, an agreeable and pleasant sight, to behold the joy of the old cat when she saw her kitten. The poor creature seemed as if she would have talked. Martha took up the kitten, and laid it on a little bit of a mat in the corner of the chimney, where it used to be; and the old cat ran to it, and lay down by it, and gave it milk, and licked it, and talked to it in her way, (that is, in the way that cats use to their kittens,) and purred so loud, that you might have heard her to the very end of the cottage. It was a pleasant sight, as I said before, for it is a pleasure to see any thing happy; and Soffrona jumped and capered about the house, and knew not how sufficiently to express her joy: and as for little Sophia, her eyes were filled with tears; and poor old Martha was not the least happy of the party.

And now, when it was time to go, Soffrona took up her empty basket, and giving the kitten a kiss, "Little Puss," she said, "I will rejoice in your happiness, though it will be a loss to me, for I must part with my little darling. But I will not be selfish: mamma says that I can never make myself happy by making other things miserable. Good-bye, little Puss: if God will help me, I will try never to be selfish." And she walked out of the cottage, wiping away her tears.

"But you will let her have Muff,

won't you, Martha," said Sophia, "when her mother has brought her up, and can part with her?"

"To be sure I will, dear Miss," replied Martha; "for I was delighted to hear her say that she knew she never could make herself happy by making others miserable."

When Muff was a quarter old, she was brought to Soffrona, and became her cat, and lived in her service till her yellow and black hairs were mingled with grey.

FINIS.

Houlstons, Printers, Wellington, Salop.

By the same *Author*.

The ORPHAN BOY. Price 6d.
A PRIMER. Price 6d.
The INFIRMARY. Price 4d.
The ERRAND-BOY. Price 4d.
The TWO SISTERS. Price 4d.
The MAY-BEE. Price 4d.
EDWARD MANSFIELD. Price 4d.
JULIAN PERCIVAL. Price 4d.
GEORGE and his PENNY. Price 2d.
EMILY and her BROTHERS. Price 2d.
The ROSE. Price 2d.
The BUSY BEE. Price 2d.
The WISHING-CAP. Price 2d.
EASY QUESTIONS. Price 2d.
ROBERT and the OWL. Price 2d.
The TWO DOLLS. Price 2d.
The SUNDAY-SCHOOL CHILD's RE
WARD. Price 1d.
LITTLE ARTHUR. Price 1d.
POOR BURRUFF. Price 1d.
The DRY GROUND. Price 1d.
The LADY in the ARBOUR. Price 1d.
The FAWNS. Price 1d.
HOME. Price 1d.

[Blank]

Appendix 1
The Illustration of Mrs. Sherwood's Work

Any representative collection of Mrs. Sherwood's tales presents a cross-section of the development of illustration in nineteenth-century children's books. On the technical side, it begins with woodcuts, used in a fashion that had not changed for centuries. Tracts, penny books, reward books, and chapbooks alike were illustrated by woodcuts; most had a frontispiece or an illustration on the title-page, and some, additional cuts scattered through the text. The frontispiece page of Houlston's penny and twopenny books carried woodcuts, usually within a rectangular or octagonal frame as in *Soffrona*. From about 1810 to 1830, in slightly larger books, the frame was sometimes surmounted by a heavy emblematic motif: in *The Little Woodman and his Dog Caesar*, for example, a Bible open in a glow of light and resting on crossed palm leaves. Depending on their length, shorter chapbooks (16–32 pages) contained from two to six little cuts with or without frames or borders. *The May-Bee* has seven little oval cuts set in heavy rectangles. The same cuts appear in more than one book; because wood-blocks were very durable, the styles depicted were often quaint and old-fashioned long before the cut went out of use.

The Whittemore tracts and Houlston's *New Series* of tracts for adults (Bibliography D1–21 and C81–93) present one fairly large cut on the title-page. Particularly fine engraving is found in Whittemore tracts printed by W. Tyler (*The Blessed Family*, *The Penny Tract*, and *Charles Lorraine*, Part I, for example); those printed by Hill carry a coarser type of work.

By the end of the century, children's books, including the much reprinted *The History of the Fairchild Family*, were usually illustrated by the glossy photographic plate, the best delicately tinted in half-tone (as in the 1913 edition). Between the two extremes lay all the refinements of wood-engraving (brought sometimes to great perfection as in Radclyffe's charming frontispiece for *The Governess*); and the copper or steel engraving favoured by publishers of the annuals and keepsakes of the 1830–50 period. The history of colour printing is likewise displayed in Mrs. Sherwood's books, particularly those published by Darton with their samples of the Baxter and Kronheim processes and the early work of Edmund Evans.

Other famous names are found in the list of artists and engravers. The neatly lettered 'O. Jewitt' on a number of Houlston's tracts is the working signature of Orlando Jewitt, well-known Victorian engraver for architectural and scientific journals. Harrison Weir, a pupil of Baxter, illustrated a great deal for Darton; William Lizars, engraver of Scottish banknotes, is represented in the printings of his countryman, Thomas Melrose, as is R. E. Bewick. William Green, the landscape artist, who wrote guide-books of the Lake District, drew the

No. 52

OF

HOULSTON'S SERIES

OF

TRACTS.

[Entered at Stationers' Hall.]

THE

TURNPIKE-HOUSE.

PART II.

BY MRS. SHERWOOD,

Author of " Little Henry and his Bearer," &c. &c.

LONDON:

PRINTED FOR HOULSTON AND CO.
65, Paternoster-Row.

Price 1d. or 7s. per 100.

[Tract Societies supplied with large quantities at a lower rate.]

(BM)

An early example of a woodcut by Orlando Jewitt, used on the cover of *The Turnpike House* (Part II). ?1826-8. (C88)

frontispiece for *The Governess*. Did he, one wonders, read the book? And if so, did it ever strike him that some governesses, including his acquaintance, the unhappy Miss Weeton (who has left in her Journal an entertaining little picture of him), led a very different sort of life from that represented by Mrs. Sherwood?

CHECK-LIST OF ILLUSTRATORS OF MRS. SHERWOOD'S
BOOKS PUBLISHED IN ENGLAND
(*Restricted to those illustrating her work during her lifetime*)

ALLEN, S. Engraver.
>Frontispieces for Darton's editions (*c.* 1840–5) of:
>*Jack the Sailor Boy*; *Grandmama Parker* . . .; *Shanty the Blacksmith*.
>? *The Lady of the Manor*, Vols. 1, 2 (Houlston, 1823–4).

BAXTER, GEORGE (1804–67). Engraver and colour printer who devised a new and expensive process of colour printing. Baxter began using it around 1829. The complicated process—which required ten to twenty wood-blocks to produce a single print—was later superseded by an easier method. Between 1829 and 1849, when Baxter began to sell licences to other printers, a number of books were illustrated by his process, among them several of Mrs. Sherwood's, all printed by Darton.

>*The Gift of Friendship* (1824). See FARRIER below.
>*Caroline Mordaunt* (1835).
>*Social Tales for the Young* (1835, 1841).
>(Handsome frontispiece, 'The Welsh Harper', is reproduced in the catalogue of the Osborne Collection.)
>*Scenes from Real Life for the Young* (1838).

BEWICK, R. E. (1788–1849). Engraver. Son of Thomas Bewick and, after 1812, his partner, Robert Elliott Bewick lacked his father's talent and originality. He was a careful designer and accurate worker.

>*The Golden Chain* (Melrose, 1829).

BRIDGES, JAMES. Landscape artist of Oxford, working between 1820 and 1853.

>*The History of the Fairchild Family*, 11th ed. (1833).

COOKE, WILLIAM BERNARD (1778–1855). Line engraver.

>*A Chronology of Ancient History* (1826), with S. Smith.
>*The History of the Fairchild Family*, 11th ed. (1833), with James Bridges.

R. E. Bewick, Sculpt.

Adelaide stripped by the gypsies in the wood.

An example of the work of Robert Bewick: the wood-engraved frontispiece to *The Golden Chain*, 2nd ed. 1830. (F2)

COOPER, J. Engraver, working for Darton.

>   *The Holiday Keepsake* (1841), with Charles Keene.
>   *The De Cliffords . . .* (1847). Eighteen full-page illustrations by Keene, engraved by Cooper.

CRAIG, WILLIAM MARSHALL (fl. 1788–1828). Miniature painter, water-colourist and drawing-master to Princess Charlotte, Craig moved from Manchester to London early in life, and became a noted designer of woodcuts in the first part of the century. His frontispieces to Mrs. Sherwood's books were engraved by William Radclyffe.

>   *The History of Lucy Clare* (1815).
>   *The Memoirs of Sergeant Dale . . .* (1816).

CRUIKSHANK, GEORGE (1792–1878).

>   *The History of Susan Gray . . .*, new edition (1828).

FAIRLAND, THOMAS (1804–52). Lithographer, portrait painter, and line engraver who engraved a number of the works of Robert Farrier (q.v.).

FARRIER, ROBERT (1796–1879). A noted Chelsea artist, portrait painter, and miniaturist. One of his specialities was, according to *The Dictionary of National Biography*, 'pictures in a slightly humorous vein depicting domestic subjects and especially scenes from schoolboy life'. Engravings on stone by Fairland of three of Farrier's paintings are found in William Darton's keepsake volume, *The Gift of Friendship* (1824); among them is a frontispiece illustrating *The Idler*.

>   (It is likely that the illustrations in *Shanty the Blacksmith* [*c.* 1835], *The Cloak* [1836], and *Scenes from Real Life* [1838], were by Farrier and Fairland.)

GREEN, WILLIAM (1761–1823). A noted landscape artist who spent much of his working life in the Lake District. He drew a number of attractive frontispieces for books printed by Houlston's, many of which were engraved by William Radclyffe.

>   *The Ayah and Lady* (1816).
>   *The History of Theophilus and Sophia* (1818).
>   *The Indian Pilgrim* (1818).
>   *The Governess, or The Little Female Academy* (1820).
>   *The History of George Desmond* (1821).
>   *The Infant's Progress* (1821).
>   *The Infant's Grave* (?1823).
>   *Père La Chaise* (1823).

JEWITT, THOMAS ORLANDO SHELDON (1799–1869). Wood-engraver. Principally an illustrator of architectural and scientific publications, Jewitt was well known in the 1850s and 1860s. Signed woodcuts by O. Jewitt appear in Houlston's *New Series* of Tracts (1821–33); in the R.T.S. volume *A Present for the Young* (*c.* 1825); and in some of Mrs. Sherwood's tracts for children printed by Houlston's in 1828.

> *New Series* 1–4: *The Young Forester.*
> 31–2: *Joan, or Trustworthy.*
> 41–2: *The Cottage in the Wood.*
> 51–2: *The Turnpike House.*
> *The Fawns* (1828).
> *Home* (1828).

KEENE, CHARLES S. (1823–91). Artist and illustrator. Thought to be one of the best comic artists of his time, Keene worked for the *London Illustrated News*, for *Punch*, and illustrated for a number of publishers, including Macmillan, Bell & Daldy, and Darton.

> *The Holiday Keepsake* (1841). See COOPER above.
> *The De Cliffords* (1847). See COOPER.

KRONHEIM, JOSEPH MARTIN (1810–96). After apprenticing with Baxter, Kronheim took out a licence in 1850 for the Baxter process of colour printing. His career as an art printer began about 1856. A pleasing example of his work is found in: *The Story of Little Henry and his Bearer Boosy*, the copyright edition, illustrated (Houlston & Wright, 1866) and in other volumes of this series.

LIZARS, WILLIAM HOME (1788–1859). Scottish painter and engraver who lived in Edinburgh. He engraved plates of Scottish scenery, anatomical plates for a medical text by his brother, and later perfected a method of etching to replace wood-engraving in book illustration. He was among the founders of the Royal Scottish Academy. Lizars's illustrations for Mrs. Sherwood's books are in those published by Thomas Melrose of Berwick. He also illustrated Scott's *Tales of a Grandfather* (1829) and Catherine Sinclair's *Holiday House* (1844).

> *The Butterfly* (1829).
> *The Father's Eye* (1830).
> *Obedience* (1830).
> *The Useful Little Girl and . . .* (1830).
> *Emmeline* (1832).
> *My Godmother* (1833).
> *The Rosary* or *Rosée . . .* By Mrs. Kelly. (1833).
> *Saint Hospice* (1835).
> *The Violet Leaf* (1835).
> (The illustrations for the above are also found in *The Garland*; the other engraver represented is Clark.)

MARCHANT, J. (op. 1840). 'Chiefly a subject-painter but often combined with landscape' (*Dictionary of British Painters,* Lewis, 1952).
Shanty the Blacksmith. A Tale of Other Times (London: Darton & Clark, n.d. *c.* 1840). Frontispiece and vignette.

MILLS, ALFRED (1776–1833). Wood-engraver, who did a good deal of illustrating for Darton & Harvey. His speciality was illustration for children's books and books of natural history.

The Hedge of Thorns (London: J. Hatchard, 1819).

RADCLYFFE, WILLIAM (1783–1855). Line-engraver. Considered one of the best engravers of the century, William Radclyffe was the founder of the Birmingham School of Art. He engraved a number of frontispieces for books printed by Houlston's (see note on William Marshall Craig and William Green above). Illustrations known to have been engraved by Radclyffe for Mrs. Sherwood's books include the following:

With WILLIAM GREEN:
The Ayah and Lady (1816).
The History of Theophilus and Sophia (1818).
The Indian Pilgrim (1818).
The Governess, or The Little Female Academy (1820).
The History of George Desmond (1821).
The Infant's Progress (1821).
The Infant's Grave (?1823).
Père La Chaise (1823).

With WILLIAM MARSHALL CRAIG:
The History of Lucy Clare (1815).
The Memoirs of Sergeant Dale (1816).

William Radclyffe also engraved the frontispiece for *Stories Explanatory of the Church Catechism* (1817) from a picture by an artist who might be William Green; and from the illustration by S. Smith, the frontispiece for *The Millennium* (1829). The revised edition of *The History of Susan Gray* (Houlston, 1818) bore a plate engraved by Radclyffe.

William Radclyffe's son, Edward Radclyffe, also an engraver, did much work for annuals in the 1840s.

SEARS, M. U. Engraver.

The Golden Garland of Inestimable Delights (Hatchard, 1849).
Scripture Prints . . . (Seeley and Burnside, 1831).

SMITH, S. Artist.

Histoire du Petit Henri (Houlston, 1820).
The Orphans of Normandy . . . (Hatchard, 1822).
A Chronology of Ancient History (Longmans et al., 1826).
Frontispiece.
Susannah, or The Three Guardians (Longmans et al., 1827).
The Millennium . . . (Hamilton Adams; Mozley & Son et al., 1829).
[Smith also illustrated for Ann Fraser Tytler's Leila (1841) and Leila in England (1842), both published by Hatchard.]

WEIR, HARRISON (1824–1906). Artist. Apprenticed for a time to Baxter, Weir became a favourite illustrator of bird and animal books for children. He was a founder of the Cat Show. An early example of his work is found in Brotherly Love (1851). The four plates reproduced in this book had been used four years earlier in Green's Nursery Annual (1847).

WILLIAMS, SAMUEL (1788–1853). Landscape artist and wood-engraver who worked on many books for children including an 1822 edition of Robinson Crusoe; Mrs. Trimmer's Natural History (1823–4); and a number of Mrs. Sherwood's.

The Nun (Seeley et al., 1833).
Robert and Frederick (Seeley et al., 1842).
Content and Discontent (in Green's Nursery Annual, 1847, Darton).
The History of the Fairchild Family, Part I, 21st ed. (J. Hatchard, 1858).
[Samuel Williams also illustrated Hone's Everyday Book; William Howitt's Rural Life of England; and Miller's Pictures of Country Life. It has been suggested that he did the wood-engraving for The Little Woodman and his Dog Caesar; since the cuts are not signed, this cannot be verified.]

Appendix II *The Firm of Houlston 1779–1906: its development and its varying imprints*

PERMUTATIONS OF THE FIRM	TYPICAL IMPRINTS
Bookseller, Market Square, Wellington 1779–1800: Edward Houlston (1) and his wife, Frances.	
* * * * * * * *	No printing.
	* * * * * * * * * * *
1800 – Edw. Houlston (1) died.	
1804 – Partnership of Frances Houlston and Edward Houlston (2). First printing 1805.	(1807)
	Wellington: Printed & Sold by F. Houlston & Son.
c. 1807. Agents in London included Hatchard's.	Sold also by (long list of booksellers here).
	Wellington: Printed & . . . Son. Sold also, by all other Booksellers. 1812.
	(Agents are G. and S. Robinson, Paternoster-Row in 1815/16.)
* * * * * * * * * * *	* * * * * * * * * * *
	1816/17 Addition of 'Salop' to imprint.
	Wellington, Salop: Printed and . . .; and sold by Scatcherd and Letterman, Ave-Maria Lane, London. 1819.
1821 – Thomas Houlston travelling for firm.	(Same. 1822.) 'Scatcherd and Co.'.
1824 – Fire at Wellington premises.	(Same imprint with addition of 'and all other Booksellers' after London. 1824.)
1825 – Warehouse established at 65 Paternoster Row, London. Edward Houlston (3) in charge?	Wellington, Salop: Printed by and for F. Houlston and Son. And sold at their Warehouse, 65 Paternoster Row, London. 1826. (Entered at Stationers' Hall.)
He was known as a bookseller at this address a year or two later.	(Same with addition of 'and by all booksellers' 1826. This imprint fairly constant through 1827, 1828.)

Frances Houlston died or retired. Edward Houlston (2) and Edward (3) in partnership until 1833.

and Son. And sold at their Warehouse, 65 Paternoster-Row, London. MDCCCXXIX. (Entered at Stationers' Hall.)

(Same imprint with date in Arabic numerals. 1829.)

London: Printed for Houlston and Son, 65 Paternoster-Row, and at Wellington, Salop. 1830. (Entered at Stationers' Hall.)

1833 – Death of Edward Houlston (3).
1835 – Thomas Houlston set up his own business at 154 Strand.

(Same. 1836, 1837,
Same. 1838, without 'entered at . . . Hall'.)

* * * * * * * * * * * * * * * *

1838 – Edward Houlston (2) and John Stoneman in partnership.
1840 – death of Edward Houlston (2). His widow, Ellen, assumes his share of the business.
1844 – death of Ellen Houlston. Thomas Houlston takes over her share and carries on business.

('Salop' disappears around 1840.)
London: Houlston and Stoneman, 65 Paternoster-Row. (c. 1845). (On cover, 'Printed for Houlston and Co.')
London: Printed for Houlston and Co. (dates in the 1840s).

* * * * * * * * * * * * * * * *

1856 – death of John Stoneman. Succeeded by Henry Wright. Partnership lasted until 1869, death of Thomas Houlston. Wright then left the firm.

London, Houlston and Wright, 65 Paternoster-Row. MDCCCLXVI (and dates from c. 1857–69).

* * * * * * * * * * * * * * * *

In 1868 – Thomas Houlston's son had joined the firm.

Houlston and Sons (1870s, 1880s, 1890s).

* * * * * * * * * * * * * * * *

1906 – Firm sold to Madgwick.

Madgwick and Houlston until around 1910.

* * * * * * * * * * * * * * * *

FIRM DISAPPEARED AFTER 1910

111

Appendix III

A Note on the Publishing of Mrs. Sherwood's Books in the United States

Early publication of Mrs. Sherwood's work in America was closely linked with the activities of the American Tract Societies. Her first children's tales were extremely popular. Their strict Evangelical doctrine was in perfect accord with the traditional Puritan theology underlying *The New England Primer* and the works of Bunyan, Janeway, or John Cotton. Furthermore, a well-established American missionary effort in the Orient ensured the enthusiastic reception and wide distribution of *The History of Little Henry and his Bearer*. Introduced in 1817, it reached fifteen editions by various printers within three years, among them a 6,000-copy issue by Flagg and Gould for the American Tract Society.

The closest American equivalent of F. Houlston and Son was probably Samuel T. Armstrong (later S. T. Armstrong and Crocker & Brewster) of Boston. Founded in 1805, this firm, which specialized in religious and didactic material, retained for seventy years the reputation of never having published an irreligious book. Among other publishers issuing Mrs. Sherwood's tales before 1825 were Flagg and Gould of Andover; Lincoln and Edmands of Boston; O. D. Cooke & Sons, and George Goodwin & Sons of Hartford; Gilman of Newburyport; Clark and Raser of Philadelphia; and Merrell and Hastings of Utica. A number of printings by the Babcocks and by Samuel Wood appeared around 1830.

During the 1840s, Mrs. Sherwood's books for the young lost ground with a large section of the general reading public. Many new Americans found the social context of her tales and her assumption of the rightness of a fixed social order incomprehensible or distasteful. Former servants and villagers, for instance, emigrants from the Old World, were unlikely to accept the lessons of patience and submission displayed in *The History of Susan Gray* or *The History of Lucy Clare*. Before 1850 the actual religious concepts stiffening the frail themes of such tales had been eroded by eighteenth-century deism and its offshoots, Unitarianism and Universalism, as well as by the progress of secular education.

> . . . (T)heological concepts were being gradually displaced . . . by rules for good conduct or by moral stories calculated to develop the natural virtues into habits of honesty, industry, and sobriety—all of which were judged essential to the good of American society. A comfortable code of ethics and certain fixed standards for temporal prosperity were supplanting those stern theological tenets which had demanded personal sanctity . . .
>
> (Monica Kiefer, *American Children Through their Books*, p. 226.)

112

Increasing Peter Parleyism also helped to strengthen American resistance to English and European books. By the 1860s, Mrs. Sherwood's work was competing with a large body of instructive writing by Samuel Goodrich and the realistic tales of Susanna Cummins and Louisa M. Alcott. Books depicting the conflict and raw vigour of pioneer life; the melodrama and sentiment of *Uncle Tom's Cabin* and other plantation tales; and the prismatic display of emotion in *The Wide, Wide World* all made Mrs. Sherwood's work seem tame and old-fashioned. Thus Little Henry and faithful Boosy were elbowed aside by Little Eva and faithful Uncle Tom; and, as in England, the religious book, no longer universally in demand, took refuge in the Sunday School under the protective wing of the Tract Society.

Except for Sunday reading, the little tract chapbooks gave way to descendants of the enduring *Goody Two-Shoes*, tales in which industry invariably brought its earthly reward. These passed by degrees into the Horatio Alger stereotype with its inevitable ending of material success and consequent rise in social status. Those of Mrs. Sherwood's tales which lasted longest in America extolled in addition to their religious lesson the virtues of industry and the spiritual excellence that flourished in humble life. For very little children they included *The Busy Bee*, *The Errand Boy* and *The History of Henry Fairchild and Charles Trueman*. A number of girls' school stories remained in favour: *Clara Stephens*, *Ellen and Sophia* and *Juliana Oakley* being the most popular.

Apart from the Tract Societies, the Universalists and the Millenarians in America printed Mrs. Sherwood's books or supplied a market for them. Passages in *The History of Henry Milner* and other works with a Millenarian flavour encouraged the followers of these movements to regard her as a sympathizer if not a strong supporter. In the 1830s, Harper & Brothers of New York brought out the first fifteen volumes of their sixteen-volume *Works of Mrs. Sherwood* as well as a three-volume *Roxobel*; all remained in print until past 1870. In 1869, too, paralleling the revived interest in Mrs. Sherwood's tales in England, R. B. Carter of New York published the six-volume 'Lily Series', each book containing a lengthy tract tale and several shorter ones.

Bibliography

INTRODUCTION

The aim of this Bibliography is chiefly to provide as complete a check-list as possible of Mrs. Sherwood's publications in book form—hence excluding the many articles and religious studies that appeared in *The Youth's Magazine* and were never reprinted. Even so, the quantity and the frequently ephemeral nature of many of her books present her bibliographers with many difficulties, and certain conventions have had to be modified here in order to ensure the inclusion of necessary basic information.

Because of the way in which the character of Mrs. Sherwood's writing is to some extent reflected by the firms publishing her books, it was decided that the most intelligible arrangement for the Bibliography would be by publisher rather than by date (and indeed, given the vagaries of a publisher like Darton, no date sequence can be entirely satisfactory without a very complicated series of cross-references).

Within each publisher section the books have been arranged chronologically according to the first edition, as far as this can be gauged. Details have been given of the earliest known edition, and of important subsequent English and American editions, and where there is a discrepancy between the date of entry and that of the edition described, it must be assumed that evidence has been found in contemporary book-lists, or in bibliographies such as *The English Catalogue*. Annotations have been added to explain special features omitted from the foregoing Study, and each entry has been given a serial number to allow for quick reference either from the text or from the Index.

Bibliographical details about all but the most important books have been reduced to the minimum of: date, title, and number of text pages, but location symbols have been added for readers who wish to inquire further. The abbreviations used for these are as follows:

AAS	American Antiquarian Society, Worcester, Mass.
Am Bib	Shaw, Shoemaker *American Bibliography*
Bib Nat	Bibliothèque Nationale, Paris
Block	Andrew Block *The English Novel 1740–1850.*
BM	British Museum Library
BMPL	Birmingham Public Library
Bod	Bodleian Library, Oxford
Boston PL	Boston Public Library, Mass.
CBEL	*The Cambridge Bibliography of English Literature*
Col	Columbia University. The Butler Library
Col TC	Columbia Teachers' College
Hunt	Henry Huntington Library, California
JJ	John Johnson Collection in the Bodleian Library
LC	Library of Congress, Washington, D.C.
Lond Lib	London Library

Newberry	Newberry Library, Chicago
NYPL	New York Public Library
Osb	Osborne Collection, Toronto Public Library
Parker	Parker Collection, Birmingham Reference Library
Phil	Free Library of Philadelphia
SSU	Sunday School Union
UBC	University of British Columbia
UCLA	University of California, Los Angeles
U Kansas	University of Kansas
UL	University of London
U Mich	University of Michigan, Ann Arbor
V & A	Victoria and Albert Museum Library
U Vic	University of Victoria, British Columbia
Yale	Yale University Library

As acknowledged in the Editorial Note on page v, many of the details of this Bibliography owe their existence to the work of Sister April O'Leary of Digby Stuart College of Education, Roehampton. Without her help in providing information about hitherto unknown Sherwood material, and in confirming details about some of the more obscure ephemera, the list would have been both less exact and less complete. Needless to say, however, she is in no way responsible for shortcomings in either the form of the present Bibliography or in the information given.

PART I

Mrs. Sherwood's Works: Arranged by Publisher

A: William Lane, The Minerva Press
B: Samuel Hazard of Cheap St., Bath
C: F. Houlston & Son of Wellington and London
    Section i: Books and Textbooks
           ii: Chapbooks and Penny Books
          iii: Tracts
D: Tracts published by William Whittemore of Paternoster Row
E: Tracts published by the Religious Tract Society
F: Tracts published by Thomas Melrose of Berwick-upon-Tweed
G: John Hatchard of Piccadilly
H: William Darton & Son of Holborn Hill
    Section i: Books, Shorter Tales and Annuals
          ii: Chapbooks in Penny and Twopenny Series
J: Other publishers
K: A Note on Collections of Mrs. Sherwood's Works

A: WILLIAM LANE, THE MINERVA PRESS: MRS. SHERWOOD'S FIRST PUB-
LISHER

  1795   *The Traditions.* A legendary tale. Written by a Young Lady. A1
        London: William Lane, 1795. Two vols. *BM; UCLA*

Mary Butt's first book, written at the age of eighteen and issued by subscription, the proceeds going to the salvage of Mr. Quentin's school at Reading. *The Critical Review* commented on its Romantic elements, saying it ought to have been called *The Superstitions*, but it approved the book's moral and its sentiment.

1799   *Margarita*. A Novel . . . By the author of *The Traditions* . . .   A2
Printed at the Minerva Press, for William Lane . . . 1799.
Four vols. *Yale*

B: SAMUEL HAZARD OF CHEAP ST., BATH

1802   *The History of Susan Gray*   B1
No copy is known, but an account of the book's writing is given in *The Life and Times of Mrs. Sherwood*, pp. 201–2, 357 and 434.
Mrs. Trimmer's review in *The Guardian of Education*, Vol. I (1802) has been noted in the Preface above, page x, and a note on the book's subsequent history is given below under item C2.

C: F. HOULSTON & SON OF WELLINGTON, SHROPSHIRE, AND LONDON*
Section i: Books and Textbooks

1814   *The History of Little Henry and his Bearer* . . . 139 pp. Frontis.   C1
[C. Barber] *UCLA*
The 2nd ed. was favourably reviewed in *The Salopian Magazine* (31 Jan. 1815) and recommendation made that the Hindustani terms be omitted. Houlston did not comply, for this was one of the attractions of the book. Many eds., illustrated in a great variety of styles, were subsequently published, and the following may be noted:
    1817   — Andover, Mass. . . . Flagg & Gould . . . 86 pp. Frontis. *Col*; *AAS*
    1820   *Histoire du Petit Henri* . . . Traduit de l'Anglois par R. P. Sémonin . . . Wellington . . . 146 pp. Engr. t.-p. *BM*; *Newberry*
    1866   *The History of* . . . London . . . iv, 107 pp. Frontis. [pr. Kronheim] *BM*; *Osb*
       Designated 'The Copyright Edition Illustrated' and including *The Last Days of Boosy* (item C38 below)
    1967   *Little Henry and his Bearer* by Mrs. Sherwood, and *The Last Days of Boosy* by A. MacNeil and Theophilus Smith. Worthing, Henry E. Walter Ltd. (The Evangelical Library) *UCLA*
       A modern edition in which the editor has taken Mrs. Sherwood's fictional narrators seriously.

* For details of the changes in Houlston's trading names and addresses, see Appendix II, pp. 110–111. This provides a general guide to the relationships of place and date in Houlston's imprints, and both 'Wellington' and 'London' have normally been omitted here for the first editions noted.

1815   *The History of Susan Gray* . . . 164 pp. Frontis.; t.-p. vignette.   C2
       BM; *Bod* (1816)
       [1823]   — [5] 143 pp. Frontis. woodcut. *BM* (1825)
       Advertised as a 'revised, corrected and, it is hoped, in some
       parts essentially improved' ed. of item B1, above. Since its
       publication in 1802 the book had been much pirated
       (largely by reason of its sentimental plot) and this new
       'Copyright Edition' was, in Mrs. Sherwood's own words,
       'evangelized' (*The Life of Mrs. Sherwood*, p. 498). The result-
       ant 'improved' Susan thus became a mouthpiece for Scrip-
       ture, while Susan unimproved—who continued to be
       pirated—kept her place on cottage shelves beside *Pamela*
       and *Maria Monk*.
       1825   *History of Susan Gray* . . . Portland, Printed by
              Shirley & Edwards. 174 pp. Frontis. *Phil*; *Am Bib*
              22272

1815   *The History of Lucy Clare* . . . [3] 147 pp. Engr. frontis. Rad-   C3
       clyffe. *BM*; *Osb* (10th ed.)
       Begun in 1802 as a companion piece to B1, the book was
       not finished until 1810. Mrs. Sherwood's Journal mentions
       a Calcutta printing of 1814, and the *English Catalogue* notes
       an edition *c*. 1812, but these seem to have disappeared. The
       1815 ed. was enthusiastically reviewed in *The Salopian
       Magazine* (Oct. 1815), where it was remarked that 'there is
       no class of writings more calculated to do good, than those
       which insinuate religious sentiments, without a formal
       notice thereof in the title-page'. The book had reached a
       22nd ed. by 1835 and was endlessly reprinted at least up to
       1889 for Sunday School, Cottage, and Servants' Libraries.
       1828   — Hartford: [?]. 108 pp. *LC*

1815   *The Memoirs of Sergeant Dale, his Daughter and the Orphan*   C4
       Mary . . . Third ed. 1816. 99 pp. Engr. frontis. Radclyffe.
       BM (3rd ed.); *Boston PL* (12th ed.)
       The book was first reviewed in *The Salopian Magazine* (30
       Nov. 1815), when the following comments on contem-
       porary children's literature were given: '. . . the press has
       long groaned under the heaps of unintelligible jargon, and
       flat nonsense, written designedly for youth. At present a
       new era seems about to commence—old things are passing
       away, and those who write for the capacities of children,
       have at last discovered, that common incidents well
       arranged, and common occurrences well related, are the
       most useful methods of instructing and improving the
       mind of infancy and youth. Instead, therefore, of such
       books as "Tom Thumb" and "Jack the Giant-Killer", we
       have the pleasure of being enabled to put into the hands of
       our children such books as "Lucy Clare" and "Sergeant
       Dale".'
       1821   — Boston: Samuel T. Armstrong . . . 71 pp.
              The first American ed. noted in *Am Bib* 6791

1816   *The Ayah and Lady*, an Indian story . . . Fifth ed. BM (cat.   C5
        only); *UCLA* (7th ed. 1822)
        According to Darton's *Life and Times*, this was translated
        into Hindustani by February 1813. It appeared in Dublin
        in 1816 as *The Lady and her Ayah*, an Indian Story (CBEL).
        1822   — from the third London ed. Boston, S. T. Arm-
                strong . . . *LC*; *Am Bib* 10259
        1828   — Madras, reprinted at the Church Mission Press
                [7] 76 pp. Frontis. *Parker*

1817   *An Introduction to Astronomy*. Intended for little Children . . .   C6
        vii, 56 pp. BM; *UCLA* (10th ed.)
        One of Mrs. Sherwood's school textbooks. See also items
        C10, C12, C16 below.

1817   *Stories Explanatory of the Church Catechism* . . . iv, 308 pp.   C7
        Engr. frontis. Radclyffe. *U Nott* (4th ed. 1818); *BM* (9th ed.
        1822); *UCLA* (14th ed. 1829)
        According to Darton's *Life and Times*, this was in print by
        June 1814 in Calcutta. In England, notices appeared in *The
        Monthly Magazine* (1 Aug. 1817) and in the *European
        Magazine* (Feb. 1818).
        1823   — Burlington, N.J.: David Allinson. 371 pp. *Am
                Bib* 14115
        1824   *Margaret Green*. Portsmouth: T. H. Miller. 70 pp.
                Am Bib 17972. Extracted from Story XXII

1818   *The History of Theophilus and Sophia* . . . Third ed. 127 pp.   C8
        Engr. frontis. Radclyffe. *Parker* (2nd ed. 1818); *Osb* (do.)
        1820   — Andover, Mass.: Mark Newman
                The first U.S. ed. noted *Am Bib* 3210. The book
                subsequently remained long in print in the American
                S.S.U. Tract Series under the title *The Shepherd of the
                Pyrenees*.

1818   *The Indian Pilgrim* . . . viii, 211 pp. (with glossary and 6-p.   C9
        book-list). Engr. frontis. Radclyffe. *BM*; *Newberry* (2nd ed.)
        [1828] *The Pilgrim of India*. Boston, James Loring. 110 pp.
                Am Bib 35187

1818   *An Introduction to Geography*. Intended for Little Children . . .   C10
        vii, 136 pp. BM; *Gumuchian* (5th ed. 1834)
        The book contains an advertisement for Mrs. Sherwood's
        school and describes her system of teaching by the use of
        cards, also used in C6. The pupil prepares the lesson from
        the book and then draws a card from a bag on which are
        inscribed two terms (e.g. 'An Island' and 'The Lord
        reigneth . . .'). To these the child must respond with the
        appropriate definition and the completion of the Biblical
        quotation. Three other textbooks are noted at C6, C12 and
        C16.

1818   *The Little Woodman and his Dog Caesar* . . . 106 pp. Frontis. C11
        and 8 woodcuts. *JJ*; *NYPL* (3rd ed. 1819)
        The book was announced in *The Monthly Magazine* for July
        1818. A facsimile of the 12th ed. of this book (1828), is given
        between pp. 100–101. As one of the most popular of all Mrs.
        Sherwood's stories it was extensively reprinted down to
        the present century. The following are some of the more
        noteworthy editions:
        [1826] — Philadelphia: American S.S.U. 36 pp. Wood-
                cuts. *Col*
        1841   *Le Petit Bûcheron et son Chien César* . . . Traduit de
                l'anglais par les demoiselles Catherine et Cécile
                Helsham. Toulouse: K. Cadaux. 48 pp. Couv. Ill.
                Bib Nat
        [1864?] *The Little Woodman* . . . London . . . Printed by
                Edmund Evans, Racquet Court (The Parlour
                Edition). 112 pp. Frontis., t.-p. woodcut, 11 wood-
                cuts by J. Knight. *U Nott*
                Houlston issued this edition in conjunction with
                S. W. Partridge, whose name appeared on the t.-p.
                Copies of Partridge catalogues dated 1864 are bound
                into some eds. and a copy has been found with an
                inscription dated 18 Jan. 1865.
                The text unchanged, but the illustrations a senti-
                mental Victorian adaptation of the original wood-
                cuts.
        [1869] — London: Seeley, Jackson and Halliday; S. W.
                Partridge and Co. (The Children's Friend Series).
                62 pp. Illus. J. Knight. *BM*
        1870   — London: Wm Macintosh. 32 pp. *BM*
                A penny book, advertising at the end three versions
                of Houlston's Copyright Edition at 6*d*., 1*s*., 1*s*. 6*d*.
                respectively.
        [1870?] — London: T. Woolmer. 95 pp. Coloured
                frontis. *Exeter City Lib.*
                Includes a printing of *The Good Nurse* (H.14) on
                pp. 66–95.
        [1900] — [Listed as No. 169 in the Catalogue of Calgary
                Presbyterian Sabbath School Library, given in the
                Calgary Herald, 1900]
        1901   — London: Jarrold & Sons. pp. 5–61 [of an
                edition that includes *Miss Helen's Portfolio* and *The
                Broken Bat*]. Frontis. *Bod*

1819   *A General Outline of Profane History* . . . vii, 300 pp. 4-p. C12
        book-list. *Osb*; *BM* (2nd ed. 1823)
        Third of Mrs. Sherwood's school textbooks. See also C6,
        C10, and C16.

1820   *The Governess, or The Little Female Academy* . . . iv, 250 pp. C13
        Engr. frontis. Radclyffe. *BM*; *Osb*
        The 'evangelized' edition of Sarah Fielding's *Governess*
        (discussed by J. E. Grey in another volume of 'The

Juvenile Library'). Houlston's attempted to defend Mrs. Sherwood against charges of plagiarism by explaining in the Preface to *The History of Emily and her Mother* (1826) that it was 'a modern picture set in an old-fashioned, though suitable frame' comparable to Hannah More's use of Scripture History in her *Sacred Dramas*.

1827   *The Governess, or The Young Female Academy* . . . From the Third English edition, New-York, for O. D. Cooke, Hartford. 222 pp. *Yale*; *Am Bib* 30594

1826   *The History of Emily and her Mother* . . . viii, 66 pp. Engr. frontis. *V & A* (1824); *Harvard* (3rd ed.)
    Individual publication of an excerpted portion of *The Governess*, which Houlston's had also issued in French in 1825 as *Histoire d'Emilie Nugent*.

1821   *The History of George Desmond*; founded on Facts which C14 occurred in the East Indies . . . 290 pp. Engr. frontis. Radclyffe. *BM*; *Yale*
    Published anonymously and continuing so till at least 1849.
    [1828?] — . . . Philadelphia [Listed among the Miscellaneous Books in the 1828 Catalogue of the American S.S.U. No author is given.]

1821   *The Infant's Progress from the Valley of Destruction to Ever-* C15 *lasting Glory* . . . iv, 237 pp. Engr. frontis. Radclyffe. *BM*; *Harvard* (2nd ed. 1821)
    1821 — Boston: Samuel T. Armstrong. *AAS*

1821   *Mrs. Sherwood's Primer, or First Book for Children* . . . Second C16 ed. 1822. 51 pp. Woodcuts. *Bod* (2nd ed.); *Harvard* (5th ed. 1829)
    Includes a severely revised text of *The Story of Little Margery*, first written 1806, and given in its original version in the first ed. of 1821. This is the fourth of Mrs. Sherwood's textbooks; see also C6, C10, and C12.
    1828 — Hartford: H. & F. J. Huntington. 48 pp. *Am Bib* 35188

1821   *The Recaptured Negro* . . . Second ed. 1821. 72 pp. *BM* (2nd C17 ed.); *UCLA* (12th ed. 1844)
    1821 — Boston: Samuel T. Armstrong. *UCLA*

?1822   *Blind Richard* C18

?1822   *The Village Schoolmistress* C19
    The above two books are listed at the start of the 1823 ed. of *The Lady of the Manor*, Vol. I. No copies have been traced.

1823   *The History of Little Lucy and her Dhaye* . . . [3] 151 pp. Engr. C20 frontis. and t.-p. *UCLA*; *BM* (2nd ed. 1825)
    First published in *The Youth's Magazine*, 1822.
    1824 — Boston: S. T. Armstrong. 72 pp. *Yale*

1823   *The Infant's Grave, a Story of the Northern Part of France* . . . C21
       75 pp. Engr. frontis. Radclyffe. *BM* (2nd ed. 1825); *Lond
       Lib* (do.)
       Extracted from *The Select Magazine*, 1822.

1823-9 *The Lady of the Manor.* Being a Series of Conversations on C22
       the Subject of Confirmation. Intended for the use of the
       Middle and Higher Ranks of Young Females . . . 7 vols.
       Issued at the rate of a volume a year, *The Lady of the Manor*
       consists of thirty long stories, several of which were
       written as early as 1800. Second eds. of Vols. I and II
       appeared in 1825 and the whole work was several times
       reissued. Ruskin must have approved of it, for he presented
       a young lady of his acquaintance with Vol. I (5th ed. 1841,
       now in *UCLA*). The work was savagely, but not very
       fairly, attacked by Lady Eastlake in the *Quarterly Review* . . .
       1843. She selected what is probably the worst (and shortest)
       tale for dissection in order to justify her complaint that
       Mrs. Sherwood's writing inculcated disrespect for parents,
       guardians, and upper classes of society.
       An early complete edition was published in America in
       1829 under the imprint of Towar & Hogan, Philadelphia.
       LC; Boston PL

1823   *Père La Chaise* . . . [3] 100 pp. Engr. frontis. Radclyffe. *Bod*; C23
       Harvard
       Extracted from *The Select Magazine*, 1822.

1824   *The History of Mrs. Catharine Crawley* . . . 101 pp. Engr. C24
       frontis. Adlard. *BM* (cat. only); *Parker*

1826   *The Captive in Ceylon*   C25
       No copy traced.
       1827 — New-York: O. D. Cooke & Co. *Harvard*; *U Mich*
             Contained in a volume entitled *New Stories*.

1826   *The Gipsy Babes.* A Tale of the last Century . . . 64 pp. Engr. C26
       frontis. *BM*; *UCLA*
       1827 — Philadelphia: American S.S.U. 54 pp. *Harvard*

1827   *The Pulpit and the Desk* . . . [5] 57 pp. Frontis. *Bod*; *BM*   C27

1828   *Arzoomund* . . . 101 pp. Engr. frontis. *BM* (2nd ed. 1829); C28
       UCLA (do.)
       First published in *The Youth's Magazine*, 1825.

1828   *My Aunt Kate* . . . [5] 72 pp. Engr. frontis. *BM*; *UCLA* (3rd C29
       ed. 1833)

1828   *Southstone's Rock* . . . [3] 91 pp. Engr. frontis. *BM*; *Col TC*   C30

1829   *Emancipation* . . . 150 pp. Frontis. *BM*; *NYPL*   C31

1830 *Intimate Friends.* 70 pp. Engr. frontis. *Parker; UCLA; BM* C32
      (2nd ed. 1834)

1830–1 *Roxobel, or English Manners and Customs Seventy Years* C33
        Ago . . . Three vols. Engr. frontis. *BM; Harvard*
        1831 — Three vols. New York: Harper. *Harvard; LC*

[?1830] *The Babes in the Wood of the New World . . .* Fifth ed. *Osb* C34
         (5th ed. [1865])
         Advertised by Houlston in 1833 list.
         1831 — New York: Mahlon Day. 67 pp. Woodcut. *UCLA*

[?1830] *The Stranger at Home . . . Boston PL* (5th ed. n.d.) C35
         Advertised by Houlston in 1833 list.
         1871 — In Vol. 3 of 'The Lily Series' (see K4)

[?1830–3] Preface for: *An Illustration of the Prophecy of Hosea.* By C36
           Mrs. T. Best. With a recommendatory Preface by Mrs.
           Sherwood . . .
           No copy is known of this book, which was listed at the end
           of an 1833 ed. of *Little Henry* (copy at Shrewsbury PL).

1831 *Ermina . . .* viii, 170 pp. Illus. *BM; UCLA* C37
      Extracted from *The Youth's Magazine,* 1826.
      1827 *Ermina, or The Second Part of 'Juliana Oakley'.* 108 pp.
            Philadelphia: Am. S.S.U. 1827. *BM; Am Bib* 30592
            A much reprinted story, sometimes entitled *Ermina
            in the East Indies;* or subtitled 'A Tale of Calcutta'.

1842 *The Last Days of Boosy, the Bearer of Little Henry . . .* Second C38
      edition [?1847] 186 pp. Engr. frontis and t.-p. *U Vic* (2nd
      ed.)
      [1842] *The Last Days of Boosy: or The Sequel to Henry and his
              Bearer.* ?Philadelphia: American S.S.U.; *U Mich*

?1844–58 *Sunday Entertainment.* A Collection of Little Pieces Cal- C39
          culated to teach Important Truths to the Reader . . . [9]
          43 pp. Woodcuts. *Parker*
          Extracts from *The Child's Magazine.*

Section ii: Chapbooks and Penny Books

Mrs. Sherwood's chapbooks for children, often confused with
those of Mrs. Cameron, overlap upon the homiletic tales. All
teach obedience, unselfishness, and religious duty. Some seem
designed to forward the work of the Bible Society, as for instance
The History of Emily and her Brothers, or *The History of Little George
and his Penny,* one of Mrs. Sherwood's earliest and most successful
tales for the young. Others show the benefits of a Sunday School
education or attempt to arouse pity for the less fortunate and the
physically handicapped.

Not many are as threatening as *The Little Sunday School Child's*

Reward, in which the child 'learned always to speak the truth, and never to tell a lie, because she knew that every liar has his portion in the lake that burns with brimstone and fire'. This tract, and the dismal 'obituary' of *The Wishing Cap*, were very widely reprinted and distributed for the next half-century. Because the religious lesson was so obvious, they became better known in Sunday Schools than the far more pleasant tales such as *Little Robert and the Owl* which was written about the same time.

After 1822, a good deal of Mrs. Sherwood's purely religious and didactic material was poured into *The Youth's Magazine* for which she wrote for over twenty years. By 1828 her short tales had almost ceased to be tracts, becoming instead amusing and often dramatic little narratives containing delightful animals (such as Poor Burruff, the dog who saved his little master from a cobra; or Soffrona's cat, Muff). Their general tone is reassuring and comforting; their religious lesson often allegorically presented, as in *The Honey Drop* or *The Hills*.

1816   *The History of Emily and her Brothers* . . . 30 pp. *Parker* (3rd   C40
        ed. 1818); *UCLA* (9th ed. 1822); *BM* (12th ed. 1824)
        1819 — Philadelphia: Clark & Raser [?32 pp.]. *AAS*

1816   *The History of Little George and his Penny* . . . 29 pp. *UCLA*   C41
        (12th ed.); *BM* (14th ed. 1828)
        Probably Mrs. Sherwood's first chapbook for children,
        written shortly after her return from India to raise funds for
        the Rev. Charles Cameron's Sunday School.
        1820 — Portland: Wm. Hyde. 31 pp. *Yale*

1818   *The Busy Bee* . . . 30 pp. *Parker*; *BM* (6th ed. 1822); *UCLA*   C42
        (7th ed. 1823)
        1821 — Andover. *Boston PL*

1818   *A Drive in the Coach through the Streets of London* . . . [5] 35 pp.   C43
        Woodcuts. *Osb* (3rd ed. 1819); *BM* (9th ed. 1824)
        Listed in *The Indian Pilgrim* (2nd ed. 1818). The style of the
        cuts bears a strong resemblance to that in *The Little Wood-
        man*.

1818   *The Rose*. A Fairy Tale . . . 27 pp. *Parker* (5th ed. 1821);   C44
        UCLA (6th ed. 1823); *BM* (8th ed. 1827)
        Listed in *The Indian Pilgrim* (2nd ed. 1818).
        1833 *The Rose, An Allegory*. New York: Mahlon Day. *Yale*

1819   *The Errand Boy* . . . [5] 35 pp. *BM*; *Osb* (9th ed.)   C45
        [1821] *The Errand Boy*. Boston: Lincoln & Edmands.
        33 [2] pp. Illus. *Yale*; *AAS*

1819   *The Little Sunday School Child's Reward* . . . 15 pp. *Phil* (3rd   C46
        ed. 1820); *BM* (15th ed. 1828)
        Listed in *General Outline of Profane History* (1819).

1819   *The Orphan Boy* . . . [5] 33 pp. *Bod* (3rd ed. 1819); *Osb* (8th ed.   C47
        1822)
        1821   — Boston: S. T. Armstrong and Crocker & Brew-
                ster. 36 pp. *Yale*

1819   *The Wishing Cap* . . . 29 pp. *BM* (5th ed. 1822); *Shrewsbury*   C48
        PL (7th ed. 1824); *UCLA* (do.)
        Listed in *General Outline of Profane History* (1819). An
        'obituary' tale, exemplifying the sinfulness of wishing,
        which implies dissatisfaction with circumstances ordained
        by God.
        1820   — Newburyport, Mass.: W. & J. Gilman. *AAS*
                One of several eds. published in the U.S. in 1820.
                Later revised as:
        1827   *The Wish, or Little Charles* . . . Philadelphia: American
                S.S.U. [5] 15 pp. *Phil*
                An 'Americanized' version in which reformations
                and conversions follow only upon illness, and not
                death.

1820   *Little Arthur* . . . 15 pp. *Parker*; *UCLA* (4th ed. 1824); *BM*   C49
        (6th ed. 1826)

1820   *The May-Bee* . . . [7] 29 pp. *Bod*; *Osb* (2nd ed. 1821)   C50
        Perhaps an attempt by Mrs. Sherwood to 'evangelize' the
        cockchafer episode in *Sandford and Merton*.
        1820   — . . . American Tract Society. 16 pp. *BM*; *UCLA*
                (*c.* 1829)

1821   *Little Robert and the Owl* . . . 31 pp. Frontis. *UCLA*; *Shrews-*   C51
        bury PL (5th ed. ?1824)
        1824   — Boston: Samuel T. Armstrong . . . 20 pp. Wood-
                cut. *UCLA*
        1868   — Reprinted in *The Children's Friend*, August and
                September 1868.
        1905   — [included as one of the stories in *Old Fashioned
                Tales*. Selected by E. V. Lucas. London: Wells,
                Gardner & Co. 1905]

1822   *Easy Questions for a Little Child* . . . 47 pp. *BM* (10th ed. 1829)   C52
        The 4th ed. was listed in an 1822 printing of *Little Henry*.
        The last of this early group of chapbooks, followed by an
        interval during which Mrs. Sherwood wrote copiously for
        The Youth's Magazine and produced the many tracts for
        Whittemore and Houlston noted below in sections C iii
        and D.

1826   *Julian Percival* . . . 35 pp. *Parker*; *Harvard*   C53
        1827   — Salem: Whipple and Lawrence. *Rosenbach*; *Boston
                PL*

1826   *The Two Dolls* . . . 31 pp. Woodcuts. *BM*; *Osb* (3rd ed. 1830)   C54

1829   *The Orange Grove* . . . 29 pp. *Bod*; *UCLA*   C69
      1842   — New York: Protestant Episcopal S.S.U. *Harvard*

1830   *Katherine Seward* . . . 36 pp. *Osb*; *UCLA* (2nd ed. 1833)   C70
      1832   — New York: N. B. Holmes
      Listed as 'with *The Well-Timed Dream* by J.A.C.' by
      Hamilton Sinclair, *Early American Book Illustrators*,
      under works illus. by R. W. Weir.

[?1830]   *The Hidden Treasure* . . . 15 pp. *Parker* (1837); *UCLA* (n.d.)   C71

[?1830]   *A Mother's Duty* . . . *Parker* (1837); *UCLA* (n.d.)   C72

[?1830]   *The Stolen Fruit* . . . 15 pp. *Parker* (1838); *UCLA* (3rd ed.   C73
n.d.)
      Extracted from *The Children's Magazine*, 1824.

1831   *Everything Out of its Place* . . . 31 pp. *Osb*   C74

1838   *The Bible* . . . 15 pp. *Parker*; *JJ* (1847)   C75

1838   *The Happy Family* . . . 15 pp. *Parker*; *Osb*   C76

1838   *The Little Negroes* . . . 15 pp. *Parker*; *Osb* (3rd ed. 1846)   C77
      Extracted from *The Children's Magazine*, 1834.

[?1833]   *A Visit to Grandpapa* . . . 31 pp. *Osb* (2nd ed.)   C78
[?]   — New York: *AAS*

Section iii: Tracts

Between 1818 and 1830, Mrs. Sherwood wrote about a hundred
tracts which were printed by at least half a dozen firms. Ranging in
length from the penny book for children to the ninety-eight page
Hedge of Thorns, they were directed to all ages and classes of
readers. Those intended primarily for servants and villagers were
sufficiently simple in style to find their way (like *The Shepherd of
Salisbury Plain*) into books for children.

Mrs. Sherwood had herself enormously extended the range of
the tract when, in 1802, she brought out *The History of Susan Gray*
with its artful use of sentiment and description. Before 1816, however, the novel was under attack from the Evangelicals; and Mrs.
Sherwood, returning from India with her gloomy experiences
fresh in her mind, had no immediate inclination towards romance.

Her domestic tracts, like those of Mrs. Trimmer and Hannah
More, are concerned with the central problems of moral reform
and spiritual redemption, and work on the earthly level towards
the restoration or maintenance of a stable social order. Those
intended for servants emphasize in the name of religion qualities
of honesty, duty, or industry. Tracts for villagers carry the usual
lesson of sobriety, patience, or resignation as stressed in the Cheap
Repository Tracts. The tone of this material varies from the harsh
Calvinism of *The Infirmary*, *The Iron Cage*, or *The Two Sisters*, to the
tearful sentiment of *Mary Anne* or *Le Fevre*, strongly reminiscent
of Legh Richmond's *Annals of the Poor* (1810–14).

About 1821, Houlston's started the *New Series* of *Religious*

Tracts. By 1822, the list of current printings contained the first eleven priced at a penny each or seven shillings the hundred and including five tracts by Mrs. Sherwood and five by Mrs. Cameron. By 1833, the series consisted of ninety.* They sold in parts or by the hundred at the same prices as in 1822, or in three bound volumes at three shillings and sixpence each, thirty tracts to a volume. Of the ninety, Mrs. Sherwood had written twenty-two under thirteen different titles. One title consisted of four separate tracts; six were two-part tracts; the remaining six were single. All remained in print till past 1875.

The *New Series* was undated. Those containing a signed woodcut by O. Jewitt were presumably printed about the same time as the children's penny books illustrated by the same artist: 1828. Otherwise the suggested dates depend upon Houlston's book-lists found in the 1822 and 1833 editions of *The History of Little Henry and his Bearer* and books published between these years.

Houlston's *New Series* were about 10 × 16·5 cm in size and from 12 to 18 pages long. Each had a woodcut on the title-page. Bound volumes as well as single tracts are to be found in a number of larger libraries, including the British Museum and the Library of Congress.

Tracts Printed Earlier than the 'New Series':

[?1817]   *The Infirmary* . . . 35 pp. *Bod* (3rd ed. 1818); *Osb* (*c*. 1875)   C79

[?1819]   *The Two Sisters* . . . 34 pp. *Bod* (3rd ed. 1820); *Phil*   C80
       Not to be confused with the book *Ellen and Sophia* (which is
       subtitled either *The Broken Hyacinth* or *The Two Sisters*). The
       tract is an unrelieved picture of the effects of drink and
       pride on the lives of the two sisters, Ann and Jane.
       1820 — Philadelphia: Clark and Raser. *Am Bib* 3213; *Phil*
       No. 127 of American Tract Society List, 1828.

Tracts in the 'New Series':

[?1821–2]   Nos. 1–4 *The Young Forester*, Pts. I–IV . . . *Bod*; *BM*   C81

[?1821–2]   No. 5 *The China Manufactory* . . . *Shrewsbury PL*   C82
       Titles above appear in 1822 book-list.

[?1822]   Nos. 19–20 *The Bitter Sweet*, Pts. I–II . . . *BM*; *Shrewsbury*   C83
       PL

[?1822–5]   No. 21 *Common Errors*   C84
       A tract of this name appears anonymously in the R.T.S.
       lists of 1849 (No. 172). In the American Tract Society
       Catalogue of 1859, *Common Errors* (No. 162) is ascribed to
       W. F. Floyd, England.

* A few years later others were added: e.g. No. 97, *The Railroad* by Mrs. Cameron, probably a tract of the 1840s.

[?1823-7]   Nos. 23-4 *Old Times*, Pts. I-II . . . BM; *Shrewsbury PL*   C85

[?1826-8]   Nos. 31-2 *Joan, or Trustworthy*, Pts. I-II . . . BM; *Shrews-*   C86
bury PL

[?1826-8]   Nos. 41-2 *The Cottage in the Wood*, Pts. I-II . . . Wood-   C87
cuts, Jewitt. BM; *Shrewsbury PL*

[?1826-8]   Nos. 51-2 *The Turnpike House*, Pts. I-II . . . Woodcuts,   C88
Jewitt. BM; *Shrewsbury PL*

[?1826-30]   Nos. 61-2 *The Hop-Picking*, Pts. I-II . . . BM; *Shrews-*   C89
bury PL

[?1826-30]   No. 67 *Do Your Own Work*. BM; *Shrewsbury PL*   C90

[?1826-30]   No. 71 *Do What You Can*. BM; *Shrewsbury PL*   C91

[?1826-30]   No. 72 *False Colours*. BM; *Shrewsbury PL*   C92

[?1826-30]   No. 81 *It is Not My Business*. BM; *Shrewsbury PL*   C93
The whole set of 90 tracts is listed in the 1833 book-list,
found in the 1833 editions of *Little Henry*. A few others were
added later, but none by Mrs. Sherwood. American printings of items C79-C83 and C85 above appeared in Vols. 8
and 13 of *Works* (see K1).

Tracts Assumed to be Later than the 'New Series'

1830   *The Oddingley Murders** 18 pp. *Bod*; UCLA (2nd ed. 1830)   C94

1830   *Sequel to the Oddingley Murders*. 18 pp. BM (cat. only)   C95

1830-1   *Hard Times*. 34 pp. UCLA   C96

[?1833]   *The Ball and the Funeral*. Philadelphia: Latimer & Co.,   C97
with *Common Errors* and *Edward Mansfield*. NYPL
Known to exist only in this American printing.

D: TRACTS PUBLISHED BY WILLIAM WHITTEMORE OF 62 PATERNOSTER
ROW, IN CONJUNCTION WITH WIGHTMAN & CRAMP AND
F. HOULSTON AND SON.

The tracts have been placed under the name of Whittemore because he was the constant factor in the publishing venture, and
Mrs. Sherwood seems to have dealt directly with him.
William Whittemore was a close neighbour in Paternoster Row
to Houlston's, whose Warehouse was opened at No. 65 in 1825.

* Mrs. Sherwood's brother, Martyn Butt, was Rector at Oddingley.
His predecessor in the parish had been murdered in 1806 over a
demand for tithes. The body of the suspected murderer (who had
disappeared) was unearthed in 1829 or 1830, and the whole case
reopened.

Between 1820 and 1829, Whittemore published a whole series of Mrs. Sherwood's and Mrs. Cameron's tracts (editions of 5,000 by 1824). In 1823, he paid Mrs. Sherwood on one occasion £15 for tracts. A heavy concentration of these in 1824, and the fact that some carry a conspicuous Houlston imprint in addition to Whittemore's, suggest that the two firms had entered into a partnership of convenience while F. Houlston and Son recovered from the damaging effects of a fire in the Wellington print shop in March 1824.

Most of the earlier Whittemore tracts were produced in conjunction with Wightman and Cramp (abbreviated here to W. & C.). The series (undated) probably began in 1820. Like most of the others, it reverted to Houlston about 1830, when Whittemore's imprint disappears. The series was sold by Seeley, Hatchard, and Nisbet in London, and by Houlston and other provincial booksellers.

These tracts were printed in America very soon after their first appearance in London, usually by S. T. Armstrong and Crocker & Brewster of Boston, and by the Sunday School Unions (see Appendix III).

Charles Lorraine, The Little Beggars, and *The Potter's Common* (in America, *The Happy Choice*) were the most widely reprinted. *Waste Not, Want Not* was among books put out by the Religious Tract Society in 1879 for servants' libraries.

All tracts listed below are 'printed for W. Whittemore', the chief firms or printers associated with him being mentioned by name. In all instances, the place of publication is London. Every tract (15 to 23 pages in length) is numbered at the bottom right-hand corner of the woodcut on the title-page. This numbering does not correspond to the order of the dating, which is so far only tentative and has been established on the basis of copies known to have existed recently or to still exist.

[?1820] *The Nursery Maid's Diary* . . . (with W. & C.). *BM* (cat. D1
only); *CBEL*

[?1820] No. 23 *Procrastination, or The Evil of Putting Off* . . . 23 pp. D2
Bm PL; *CBEL*
1829 *Procrastination, or The Evil of Delay* . . . New York:
General Protestant Episcopal S.S.U. *Boston PL*

[?1820] No. 24 *The Young Mother* . . . (with W. & C.) 16 pp. *Block*; D3
Bm PL (3rd ed.) [1973. Now known to be by Mrs. Cameron.]

[?1820] No. 27 *The Iron Cage* . . . (with W. & C.) 16 pp. *V & A*; D4
JJ
1842 — New York: General Protestant Episcopal S.S.U.
23 pp. Illus. *Harvard*

[?1820] Nos. 41–2 *The Golden Clew*, Parts 1–2 (with W. & C.) D5
Block; *JJ* (*c.* 1830)
1831 — Boston: James Loring. *Phil*

1821 Nos. 5–9 *Charles Lorraine, or The Young Soldier* . . . (with D6
     (W. & C.) 16–16–16–17–19 pp. *V & A*; *UCLA*
     Favourably reviewed in *The Evangelical Magazine*, 1821.
     1823   — Boston: S. T. Armstrong and Crocker & Brew-
            ster. 72 pp. *Phil; NYPL*

[?1822–3] No. 1 *The Penny Tract* . . . (with Houlston) 20 pp. *BM*; D7
     LC (1824)
     1823   — Boston: S. T. Armstrong and Crocker & Brew-
            ster. 20 pp. *Phil; Col TC*

[?1822–3] No. 11 *The History of Mary Saunders* . . . 16 pp. *V & A*; D8
     NYPL (1830)
     By 1830, printed by Houlston.
     1823   — Boston: S. T. Armstrong, etc. 16 pp. *Harvard*

[?1822–3] No. 13 *The Blind Man and Little George* . . . (with W. & D9
     C.) 15 pp. *V & A*; *BM* [?1824]
     1823   — Boston: S. T. Armstrong, etc. 16 pp. *NYPL*

1822–3 Nos. 15–18 *The Potter's Common, or The Happy Choice*, D10
     Pts. 1–4 (with Houlston). 18–16–16–16 pp. *BM*; *Bm PL*
     (with W. & C.), Pts. 1–3, n.d.; Pt. 4, Whittemore, 1824.
     V & A; *Parker*
     [?1828]   — Am. S.S.U. (cat. 1828). 69 pp. *Phil; Yale* (1830);
            UCLA (1830)

1822–3 *The Poor Man of Colour, or The Sufferings* . . . *BM* (cat. only, D11
     ?1830)

1823 [?earlier] No. 2 *The Blessed Family* . . . (with Houlston, 1824, D12
     4th ed.) 16 pp. *BM* (4th ed.); *V & A* (do.)
     1823   — Boston: S. T. Armstrong, etc. 16 pp. *NYPL*;
            UCLA

1824 *Content and Discontent* . . . (with Houlston) 16 pp. *V & A* D13

[?1824] No. 28 *The Lambourne Bell* . . . (with W. & C.) 20 pp. *BM*; D14
     V & A; *NYPL*; (with Houlston)

1824 Nos. 29–30 *The Little Beggars*, Pts. 1–2 . . . (with W. & C.) D15
     36 pp. *BM*; *CBEL*
     By 1830, printed by Houlston.
     c. 1830   — Am. S.S.U. *BM*
            Also appears under alternative title of *The Children
            of the Hartz Mountains.*

1824 Nos. 35–8 *Waste Not Want Not*, Pts. 1–4 . . . (with W. & C.; D16
     later with Houlston) 20–16–16–18 pp. *V & A*; *BM*

1829 *The Little Orphan* . . . Listed *Block* D17

1829   *Little Sally* . . . Listed *Block*   D18
       c. 1836   — Am. S.S.U. 3rd series

[1829]   The following titles have been taken from a list of these
         tracts advertised by Houlston and Stoneman (i.e. 1838–45).
         Copies have not been found anywhere to date.
         Nos. 45–6 *The Crows' Nest*   D19
         No. 47 *Darkwood Court*   D20
         No. 48 *The Apprentice*   D21

E: TRACTS PUBLISHED BY THE RELIGIOUS TRACT SOCIETY, FOR THE
   DEPOSITORY, PATERNOSTER ROW; FOR J. NISBET, BERNERS ST.; AND
   OTHER R.T.S. BOOKSELLERS

[?1820–5]   *Abdallah, the Merchant of Bagdad* . . . 30 pp. Woodcuts.   E1
            Phil

[?1820–5]   *The Fountain of Living Waters* . . . 30 pp. Woodcuts. *BM*   E2
            (?1825)
[?1820]   *Mary Anne* . . . 36 pp. Woodcuts. *BM* (?1820; 2nd ed.   E3
          ?1823); *Osb* (4th ed.)
          1831   — New York: Pendleton & Hill. *UCLA*
                 Bound with *The Red Book* (E5 below).

1827   *The Two Sisters, or Ellen and Sophia* . . . 108 pp. Woodcuts.   E4
       BM; *Osb*
       First printed in *The Youth's Magazine*, 1827, where it is sub-
       titled *The Broken Hyacinth*.
       1828   — Am. S.S.U. (No. 502, Last Series, cat. of 1829)

1830   *The Red Book* . . . 34 pp. Woodcuts. *UCLA*; *Bod* (3rd ed.   E5
       1833); *BM* (4th ed. 1836)
       First published in *The Youth's Magazine*, 1829.
       1831   — New York: Pendleton & Hill (with *Mary Anne*).
              UCLA; *Phil* (1833)

1830   *The Flowers of the Forest* . . . 108 pp. Woodcuts. *BM*; *UCLA*   E6
       1833   — Philadelphia: George Latimer and Co. 104 pp.
              Phil; *NYPL*
              Known also in America as *The Lily of the Valley*.

[1825]   [*My Father and his Family.*] In *A Present for the Young*,   E7
         London. *BM*; *Cutt*
         Not signed; but assumed on the evidence of style, content,
         names of persons, etc., to be by Mrs. Sherwood. At this
         date, the R.T.S., whose policy was to buy copy outright,
         did not encourage its authors to declare themselves.

F: TRACTS PUBLISHED BY THOMAS MELROSE OF BERWICK-ON-TWEED

Little is known of the publishing activities of Thomas Melrose,
who began his forty-year career as a businessman in Berwick-on-
Tweed about 1827. Like William Whittemore earlier, he shared his

132

titles with Houlston's (to which most of them reverted by 1840). Printing was not his sole concern, to judge by the amusing array of sidelines listed in *Pigot's Directory* of 1858:

'Melrose and Plenderleith, High Street. Booksellers, publishers, stationers, printers, bookbinders, music-sellers, British and Foreign Bible Society's Depository, and agents for Horniman's Tea.'

By 1868, however, Plenderleith had gone (so had the music, the Depository, and the Horniman's Tea); and after that year Thomas Melrose too disappears from the pages of *Pigot*.

Forty years before, he had published the first of his twenty-two titles by Mrs. Sherwood. A number of them are rare today except in Harper's sixteen-volume edition of her collected *Works*, where they appear in volumes 7, 13, and 14. In 1835, seventeen tales were published in a collection entitled *The Garland* (F22) which was widely advertised in Scottish religious periodicals. Less decorative than Darton's collections, but more substantial in content, it was brought out jointly by Melrose and Houlston, and contained a number of engravings by William Home Lizars. Most of these tales appear in *Works* (K1).

Where a *Garland* copy has been located here, the location has been followed by a (G).

1829   *The Butterfly* . . . 45 pp. Engr. Lizars. *Bod*(G); *UCLA*   F1

1829   *The Golden Chain* . . . 85 pp. 4 Woodcuts, R. E. Bewick.   F2
       Parker; *Bod*(G); *UCLA*
       Reviewed in Edinburgh *Literary Journal*, Oct. 1829.

1830   *The Father's Eye* . . . [5] 40 pp. Engr. frontis. Lizars. *Harvard*;   F3
       BM (1833)

1830   *The Mountain Ash* . . . [5] 36 pp. 3 Engrs., R. Clark. *Bod*(G);   F4
       Parker (2nd ed. 1832); *Boston PL*

1830   *Obedience* . . . 87 pp. Engr. frontis. Lizars. *BM* (2nd ed. 1831);   F5
       Gumuchian
       First published in *The Youth's Magazine*, 1828.

1830   *The Two Paths, or The Lofty and The Lowly Way* . . . 41 pp.   F6
       Engr. frontis. *Bod*(G); *Col TC*; *UCLA* (also 4th ed. 1835)
       1839   *The Lofty and The Lowly Way* . . . New York: John S.
              Taylor. 25 pp. *NYPL*. Taylor also published an
              edition in 1839 which included F7, F11 and F13
              below; *UCLA*

1830   *The Useful Little Girl and The Little Girl Who was of no Use*   F7
       at all . . . [5] 41 pp. Engr. frontis. Lizars. *Parker*
       1839   — New York: John S. Taylor, with *The Lofty and the
              Lowly Way*. *UCLA*. See also F6

1832   *Emmeline* . . . Engr. Lizars. *Bod*(G); *UCLA*   F8

1833   *Aleine, or Le Bächen Hölzli* . . . 40 pp. Engr. frontis. *Bod*(G);   F9
        Harvard (2nd ed. 1833)

1833   *The Convent of St. Clair* . . . 74 pp. BM (cat. only); *Bod*(G)   F10

1833   *My Godmother* . . . 38 pp. Engr. frontis. Lizars. *Bod*(G);   F11
        UCLA. See also F6

1833   *The Rosary, or Rosée de Montreux* . . . Engr. frontis. Lizars.   – –
        Parker; *Bod*(G)
        Usually printed as Mrs. Sherwood's, this tale is actually her
        daughter's, as is *The Drooping Lily*. See note on Sophia
        Kelly on pp. 94–5.

[1834–5]   *The Basket-Maker* . . . *Bod*(G)   F12
        Found so far only in *The Garland*; but since Harper printed
        it in the *Works* in 1834, it must have come out no later than
        that year.
        1839   — New York: J. S. Taylor (bound with *The Drooping
            Lily*). *UCLA*

1835   *The Red Morocco Shoes* . . . *Bod*(G)   F13
        See item F12 above.
        1839   — New York: J. S. Taylor. See also F6

1835   *The Roman Baths, or The Two Orphans* . . . 73 pp. Engr. frontis.   F14
        UCLA

1835   *Saint Hospice* . . . Engr. frontis Lizars. *Bod*(G)   F15

1835   *The Violet Leaf* . . . Engr. frontis. Lizars. *Bod*(G); *Gumuchian*   F16
        First published in *The Youth's Magazine*, 1830.

1836   *The Last Request of Emily* . . . 38 pp. Engr. frontis. *Osb* bound   F17
        with F18

1836   *The Well-Directed Sixpence* . . . 38 pp. Frontis. *Osb* bound   F18
        with F17

1836   *The School Girl* . . . 38 pp. Frontis. *Osb*   F19
        Includes a list of 21 titles by Mrs. Sherwood published by
        Melrose.

1837   *The Parson's Case of Jewels* . . . ix, 247 pp. Frontis. *BM*   F20
        First published in *The Youth's Magazine*, 1834. The *English
        Catalogue* lists a printing by Longmans in Dec. 1836, but
        this has not been traced. Also Houlston, 1849. The sequel—
        The [Parson's] Jewel-Case Re-opened (*Youth's Magazine*, July–
        Dec. 1841) was later extracted for printing in book form.
        Allibone states 'new ed. 1849' but does not give the pub-
        lisher.

134

1839 *The Indian Orphans.* A narrative of facts including many F21
notices of the Rev. Henry Martyn, B.D., and the Right Rev.
Daniel Corrie, Lord Bishop of Madras . . . [with Houlston?]
Scottish National Library, Edinburgh
Reprinted by Longmans, 1840, and Simpkin, 1849, this
book is an account of Mrs. Sherwood's work on behalf of
the regimental orphans during her ten years in India. Most
of the material is covered by the Journal as edited by Sophia
Kelly.

1835 *The Garland. A Collection of Moral Tales* . . . 312 pp. Plates. F22
Bod

G: BOOKS AND TRACTS PUBLISHED BY JOHN HATCHARD OF PICCADILLY,
LONDON

1818 *The History of the Fairchild Family: or The Child's Manual:* G1
being a collection of stories calculated to shew the importance and
effects of a religious education . . . Printed for J. Hatchard,
190 Piccadilly; and sold by F. Houlston and Son, Wellington. [8] 302 pp. Frontis. *BM; Parker; UCLA*
The first part of Mrs. Sherwood's most famous story.
Parts 2 (1842) and 3 (1847) have been included in the following synopsis of significant subsequent editions, abridg-
ments and excerpts, which has been given its own numbered sequence for ease of reference.

1819 — The fourth edition, corrected. *BM*   G1.1
1828 — In two volumes. New York: W. Burgess, jun. G1.2
Frontis. *UCLA; Phil* (Vol. I); *Yale* (Vol. II)
1833 — Eleventh edition. J. Hatchard & Son. 300 pp.   G1.3
Engr. frontis. W. Cooke, jun., after Bridges. *U Vic*
1839 *Die Familie Fairschild* . . . nach der französischen G1.4
Uebersetzung deutsch bearbeitet. Düsselthal,
Rettungs-Anstalt. viii, 425 pp. Lith. frontis. and
5 illustrations, W. Severin. *BM*
Includes a translation of the original French
preface by A. Rochart, dated 1834. No copy
of this French ed. has been traced.
1842 — Part II. John Hatchard & Son. 359 pp. Frontis. G1.5
BM; Bod
1847 — Part III. John Hatchard & Son. 352 pp. Engr.   G1.6
Frontis. *Bod* (with 36 pp. Hatchard cat.)
In a brief Preface Mrs. Sherwood acknowledges
her daughter who 'has been of especial service to
me'.
1845–7 — Three volumes   G1.7
The first uniform edition, a further edition appearing in 1868.
1852 *Histoire de la Famille Fairchild.* Traduit de l'anglais. G1.8
Paris, Lib. Protestant de Grassart. Three volumes.
Harvard
[1875] *The History of the Fairchild Family* [Pt. I]. London: G1.9
Ward, Lock & Tyler. vi, 213 pp. *BM; Bod* (1879)

1875–6 — [One volume edition of Pts. I–III] Hatchard. G1.10
572 pp. Illust. *BM*; *Bod*
[?1875] — [Pt. I] London: Ward, Lock & Co. (The G1.11
Home Treasure Library), viii, 300 pp. Coloured
frontis. *Bod*; *NYPL*
[?1889] — [One volume edition of Pts. I–III] London: G1.12
J. Nisbet & Co. 542 pp. Illust. *BM*
[1902] — edited with an introduction by Mary E. Pal- G1.13
grave. With illustrations by Florence M. Rudland
[Pts. I and II] London: Wells, Gardner, Darton &
Co. xxxii, 469 pp. *BM*; *Osb*
[1908] — Retold by Jeanie Lang. Pictures by Evelyn G1.14
Beale [Pts. I, II abridged] London and Edinburgh:
T. C. & E. C. Jack (Grandmother's Favourites).
111 pp. 8 plates. *BM*
1913 — Edited and abridged by Lady Strachey. Con- G1.15
taining eight full-page illustrations in colour by
Miss Sybil Tawse [Pts. I and II] London: A. & C.
Black, vii, 354 pp. *BM*; *LC*

Excerpts from the *Fairchild Family*:

1821 *The History of Henry Fairchild and Charles Truman.* G1.16
Boston: Samuel T. Armstrong and Crocker &
Brewster. 36 pp. *Boston PL*; *Phil*
A popular excerpt in the U.S., subsequently pub-
lished also in New York (1822), Utica (1824), and
Philadelphia [?1828].
1908 *Margot and the Golden Fish* [i.e. 'The Story of Little G1.17
Martin'; 'Edwy and the Echo'; 'The Old Story of
Mrs. Howard']. Retold by Amy Steedman. Pictures
by M. D. Spooner. London and Edinburgh: T. C.
& E. C. Jack (Grandmother's Favourites). 96 pp.
BM
1962 ['Emily and the Damsons' abridged in] *Naughty* G1.18
Children. An Anthology compiled by Christianna
Brand. Illustrated by Edward Ardizzone. London:
Victor Gollancz Ltd., 1962, pp. 86–90
1968 'The Old Story of Mrs. Howard' [and] 'The Stolen G1.19
Child' [in] *The Hole in the Wall* and other Stories.
Edited by Gillian Avery. Illustrated by Doreen
Roberts. London: Oxford University Press, 1968,
pp. 17–47

1819 *The Hedge of Thorns* . . . 98 pp. Engr. frontis. A. Mills. *BM*; G2
Osb
1820 — New York: Samuel Wood & Sons . . . 87 pp.
Frontis. *Boston PL*; *UCLA*
1822 *The Orphans of Normandy, or Florentin and Lucie* . . . 145 pp. G3
Frontis. and 2 plates. S. Smith. *UCLA*; *BM* (2nd ed. 1822)
1827 — Hartford: D. F. Robinson & Co. 106 pp. Frontis. *Yale*; *UCLA*

1822   *The History of Henry Milner, a little boy who was not brought*   G4
        up according to the fashions of this world. [8] 187 pp. Engr.
        frontis. *UCLA; Bod* (1823); *Osb* (1823)

      1823   — Burlington, N.J.: Published by D. Allinson and
               sold by A. H. Maltby and Co., New Haven; O. D.
               Cooke & Sons, Hartford. iv, 187 pp. Frontis. *Yale;*
               Phil

      1826   — (Part 2) (Unillustrated) Hatchard. *Harvard UCLA*
               (2nd ed.)

      1831   — (Part 3) Hatchard. 469 pp. *Bod; Harvard*
      1837   — (Part 4) Hatchard. 489 pp. *Bod; Harvard*

    The History of Henry Milner was well received in America.
The Universalists found in it confirmation of their belief
that Mrs. Sherwood and Mrs. Streeten had joined their
ranks; and sent a gift of tastefully-bound books (her own)
which they had reprinted. They did not make her denials
public. *Henry Milner* was also appreciated by the Millenarians, among whom Mrs. Sherwood could certainly
be counted. But the most popular form it took in America
was a series of short extracts, usually 24 pages long,
printed in Boston and in Troy, N.Y. between [?1850] and
1857. A number of these have survived, often pleasingly
illustrated by the woodcuts of Alexander Anderson and
his pupils, and the following may be found at the Philadelphia Free Library:

    Master Henry's Arrival, and *The Alarm*
    Master Henry's Green Bag; its Loss and Recovery
    Master Henry's Lesson: The Visitors: and *Haymaking*
    Master Henry's Rabbit; The Bees; and *The Faithful Dog*
    Master Henry's Visit at Mrs. Green's; and *His Return*
    Master Henry's Walk; and *The Story of Jenny Crawley*

In 1855 these six parts were bound in a single volume,
published at Boston by Dayton & Wentworth:
    The History of Master Henry, a pleasing narrative for the
    young.

1833   *The Little Momiére.* 226 pp. Frontis. *BM; Osb*   G5
      1842   *Sophie et sa Mère, où* . . . Paris: L. R. Delay. *Bib Nat*
    A mournful little tract tale about the lack of Sabbath
    observances on the Continent. The circumstances of its
    writing are given in the *Life of Mrs. Sherwood,* p. 550.

1833   *Victoria* . . . 231 pp. 2 engrs. *BM; Harvard*   G6
      1833   — Philadelphia: J. Whetman. 272 pp. *Hunt*

1841   *Julietta di Lavenza* . . . 208 pp. *BM*   G7

1844   *The History of John Marten. A Sequel to The Life of Henry*   G8
    Milner . . . 517 pp. *BM; Yale*

1849 *The Golden Garland of Inestimable Delights.* By Mrs. Sher- G9
wood, and her daughter, Mrs. Streeten . . . 383 pp. Frontis. engr. M. U. Sears. *BM*; *Osb*
Dedicated to Lady John Somerset.

1851 *The Mirror of Maidens in the Days of Queen Bess.* By Mrs. G10
Sherwood and her daughter, Mrs. Streeten . . . 348 pp.
Frontis., engr. M. U. Sears. *BM*; *Bod*
Later claimed by Mrs. Streeten (then Mrs. Kelly) to be
mostly hers.

H: BOOKS PUBLISHED BY WILLIAM DARTON AND SON OF HOLBORN HILL,
LONDON; LATER DARTON & CLARK AND DARTON & CO.
Section i: Books, Shorter Tales and Annuals

1832 *Dudley Castle*, a Tale. 108 pp. Engr. frontis. and t.-p. vig- H1
nette. *BM* (1834); *Yale* [1834]
Earliest allusion to this work seems to be *Bent's Literary
Advertiser*, 1832, and *The British Magazine*, 1 May 1832.

1834 The *Monk of Cimiés* . . . 428 pp. Frontis. *Bod* (1836); *BM* H2
(1837)
1837 — New York: Harper. *Works*, Vol. 14 (see K1)

1835 *Caroline Mordaunt, or The Governess* . . . [2] 232 pp. Engr. H3
frontis. Baxter. *UCLA*
1853 *Caroline Mordaunt.* [ii], 214 pp. Frontis. steel engr.
BM; *NYPL*

[1835] *The Old Cobler of the Cottage*: to which is added *The Idler* . . . H4
70 pp. Frontis., 3 litho plates. *NYPL*; *V & A* (2nd ed.)
The Idler, by Mrs. Sherwood, is extracted from Darton's
Annual, *The Gift of Friendship* (1824). *The Old Cobler* is by
Mme. de Montolieu.
1837 *The Idler.* New York: Harper. *Works*, Vol. 15 (see
K1)

[1835] *Shanty the Blacksmith. A Tale of Other Times.* 2 plates engr. H5
on stone. *Gumuchian*
1838 — [Listed on cover of *Scenes from Real Life* (1838)]
1839 — New York: [?J. S. Taylor]. *AAS*
[1841] — London: Darton. 176 pp. 3 lithographs. *Osb*
Reprinted *c.* 1844 with different illustrations *BM*. After
1864, the book was being printed by Milner &
Sowerby as *The Maid of Judah*, perhaps in deference
to the current interest in Old Testament studies and
the Holy Land.

1835 *Social Tales for the Young.* 230 pp. Frontis. in colour. Baxter H6
BM; *Osb*
Of the ten stories in this volume, nine had previously
appeared in *The Youth's Magazine* (1827–33). The volume
was reprinted (augmented by *The Christmas Carol* and *Old
and New Things*); its tales were also brought out in sets of

four (*Scenes from Real Life for the Young*); and sets of two in sixpenny books. All except *The Christmas Carol* were printed by Harper in *Works*, Vol. 13 (see K1).

1835 — Philadelphia: J. Whetman. 2 plates, [4] 196 pp. *NYPL*

1841 — Darton. 247 pp. *BM*
One additional tale: *The Christmas Carol*.

1838 *Scenes from Real Life for the Young* . . . First Series. 85 pp. 4 plates, litho (sometimes in colour). *Bod*; *Osb*

1839 — Second Series
Listed *Eng. Cat.*

1850 *Family* [sometimes 'Familiar'] *Tales*. 144 pp. Frontis. *Bod*; *NYPL*
Reprint of *Social Tales* in Juvenile Library Series.

[1836–47] *The Mail Coach* and *The Old Lady's Complaint*. 64 pp. *BM* (cat. only). *Col TC*
Tentative date set by BM is 1830, which is too early for the second tale (*Youth's Magazine*, 1833).

[1836–47] *My Three Uncles* and *The Swiss Cottage*. 64 pp. *UCLA*; *Bod* (In *Family Tales*, 1850)
Tentative date of 1825 (BM) is too early.

[1836–47] *Obstinacy Punished* and *Economy*
Listed in *The Heron's Plume*, a sixpenny book of the same period, as are the next two titles. No copies have been discovered of these three books. *Economy* is the third tale in the *Scenes from Real Life* First Series.

[1836–47] *The Hours of Infancy* and *Hoc Age*

[1836–47] *The Shepherd's Fountain* and *Old and New Things*

[1839] *The Christmas Carol*. [5] 70 pp. *BM*; *Osb* (*c.* 1860)

[1841] *The Juvenile Forget-me-Not* [3] 254 pp. 4 engrs. numerous cuts. *V & A*; *Osb*   H7
One of Darton's highly illustrated annuals. Each of the four stories has an engr. frontis. and a dozen or more cuts of varying style and quality. Mrs. Sherwood wrote the stories around the cuts. Soon after their publication in the annuals, the tales were printed separately, often with an unrelated engraving, the supply of frontispieces having given out. Both annuals and tales were about 12 × 15 cm in size, cloth-bound as a rule, with gilt decorations. All were frequently reprinted.

[1842] *Think Before you Act* . . . *Phil*

[1842] *Frank Beauchamp, or The Sailor's Family* . . . [3] 64 pp. Engr. frontis., cuts. *V & A*; *NYPL*

[1842] *Grandmama Parker, or The Father's Return* . . . 64 pp. Engr. frontis., cuts. *Bod*; *UCLA*

[1842] *Uncle Manners, or Self-Will Cured* . . . 62 pp. Engr. frontis., cuts. *V & A*; *UCLA*

1844–5 *Clever Stories for Clever Boys and Girls* . . . Philadelphia and New York: Appleton. *Phil*
Contains *Think Before You Act*, *Jack the Sailor Boy*, and *Duty is Safety*.

[1841] *The Holiday Keepsake* . . . 256 pp. 4 engrs., cuts. *Bod; BM*   H8
An annual, several times reprinted, from which the follow-
ing items were extracted. The 1842 edition varies slightly
in content.

[1842]   *Sisterly Love* . . . 64 pp. Frontis. and cuts. *Parker*
[1842]   *Duty is Safety, or Troublesome Tom* . . . *Bod; BM* (1864)
1845   — Philadelphia and New York: Appleton. *Phil*
[1842]   *The Traveller* . . . 64 pp. Frontis., cuts. *V & A; Osb*
[1842]   *Jack the Sailor Boy* . . . 64 pp. Frontis., cuts. *Bod;*
        U Mich
[1846]   — Philadelphia and New York: Appleton. *NYPL;*
        Yale (1850)
[1845]   *The Wreck of the Walpole* . . . 32 pp. Frontis. *NYPL;*
        Bod (In *Holiday Keepsake*, 1842)

1836   *Biography Illustrated* . . . 163 pp. Frontis. and engr. *BM;*   H9
       NYPL [1839]

1836   *Contributions for Youth*. Listed *Eng. Cat.* (1836). *London Cat.* H10
       No copy known.
       A reissue of *The New Year's Token* (1835), an annual contain-
       ing stories by several writers.

[1836] *The Cloak*; to which is added *The Quilting* . . . 72 pp. 3 H11
        plates, litho. *V & A; NYPL*
        The Quilting is by Eliza Leslie. *The Cloak* is extracted from
        The New Year's Token, 1835.

1838   *Sea-Side Stories* . . . 144 pp. 4 plates, litho. *BM*
[1838]   — 98 pp. Frontis. *NYPL*   H12
        In 'The Juvenile Library' Series.

[1839] *The Little Girl's Keepsake* . . . 176 pp. Frontis. *UCLA*   H13
        A volume of the *Holiday Library Series* and later printed by
        Milner & Sowerby. Contains two tales, 'Adelaide and
        Antoinette' and 'False Kindness'. According to F. J.
        Harvey Darton, the *Holiday Library Series* 'was rushed out
        in opposition' to 'Felix Summerly's' *Home Treasury Series*
        of 1846.

[1844] *The Lost Trunk* and *The Good Nurse* . . . 32 pp. Frontis. *BM* H14
        (1877); *Bod* (1891)

[1840–7] *The Heron's Plume* [3] 64 pp. Frontis. *UCLA*   H15
        Bound with *The Quadrupeds' Pic-nic*, and *The Hog and Other
        Animals* (by Dr. Aikin). *The Quadrupeds' Pic-nic* may not be
        by Mrs. Sherwood. *The Heron's Plume* appears in various
        late Victorian collections such as the Book Society re-
        printings of 1877, and W. Swan Sonneschein's *Juvenile
        Library* (1891).

[1840–7] *The Fall of Pride* . . . 72 pp. 2 plates, 4 cuts. *Parker;* H16
        NYPL

[1840–7] *The White Pigeon* . . . 64 pp. *UCLA* [1877] H17

[1840–7] *Martin Crook* . . . *Bod* (In *Mrs. Sherwood's Juvenile* H18
Library, Vol. 2, 1880)

[1841–7] *The Joys and Sorrows of Childhood*, and *The Loss of the* H19
Rhone . . . 171 pp. *BM* [1844]; *Boston PL* [1844]

1847 *The De Cliffords*. An historical tale by Mrs. Sherwood and H20
Streeten Butt . . . 314 pp. Plates. *BM*; *Bod*; *Harvard*
The Preface by Mrs. Sherwood, dated 15 October 1846,
explains that this book is a joint effort. 'It has been further
arranged by Providence, that this daughter, Mrs. Streeten,
has inherited from me, a turn for composition.' After her
mother's death, Mrs. Streeten (by then, Mrs. Kelly) claimed
the book as her own, 'assisted by Mrs. Sherwood'.

1847 *The Keepsake*. iv, 186; ii, 214; 188 pp. Frontis., plates. H21
NYPL
Contains *A Soldier's Life*; *Caroline Mordaunt*; *Old Man's
Wanderings*. The first and last tales may not be by Mrs.
Sherwood.

1849–50 *The Young Lord and Other Tales* by Mrs. Crosland, late H22
Camilla Toulmin. Vol. 5 of Darton's *Holiday Library*. The
second tale, *Victorine Durocher, or The Blessings of Peace*, is by
Mrs. Sherwood and her daughter, Mrs. Streeten. 57–143
pp. *BM*; *Bod*

1851 *Green's Nursery Annual* . . . Published by Darton from 1847 H23
to 1858. The 1858 volume, which is a reprint of most of
1851, contains *The Harvest Home* by Mrs. Sherwood, 18–32
pp. *BM*; *Osb* (1851, 1858)

1851 *The Two Knights, or Delancey Castle*. A Tale of the Civil H24
Wars . . . vi, [3] 302 pp. Frontis. Plates. *Bod*; *BM*; *UCLA*

1851 *Brotherly Love*. Shewing that as merely human it may not H25
always be depended upon. By Mrs. Sherwood and her
daughter, Mrs. Streeten. 113 pp. 4 plates (sometimes
coloured), Harrison Weir. *Cutt. UCLA* (later ed.)
1860 — *The Brothers, or Be Not Wise in Your Own Conceit.*
London: Milner & Sowerby. No copy known.

1852 *Home Stories for the Young* . . . *Bod*; *Eng Cat* H26
Contains *Martin Crook*; *The Rose and Nightingale*; *The Fall of
Pride*; *The Heron's Plume*; [*The Hog and Other Animals*]; *The
Wreck of the Walpole*

1854 *Boys Will Be Boys, or The Difficulties of a Schoolboy's Life*. By H27
Mrs. Sherwood and her daughter, Mrs. Kelly. viii, 315 pp.
Engr. frontis. sometimes in colour. *Bod*; *Osb*

1861   *My New Story Book . . . Eng Cat; Scottish Nat Lib*   H28
       This item has not been available for examination; but is
       catalogued by S.N.L.

?1854–62   *The Golden City and Other Tales . . . Col TC*   H29
       One of a set of sixpenny titles issued after Mrs. Sherwood's
       death, and described in a Darton & Hodge book-list
       (*Brotherly Love, c.* 1862, *Osb*) as 'an entirely new series of
       Juvenile books from the unpublished MSS. of the late
       Mrs. Sherwood, edited by her daughter, Mrs. Kelly'.
       Known also as 'Mrs. Sherwood's Juvenile Library' or
       'Mrs. Sherwood's Parting Gift', they were cheaply and
       often carelessly assembled, and included tales by Sophia
       Kelly. Eight titles in all were listed.

?1854–62   *The Greedy Boy, and Grateful Dog, and Other Tales . . .*   H30
       Col TC

?1854–62   *Must I Learn, and Other Tales* . . . Frontis. chromo-   H31
       litho. Cuts. *V & A; Eng Cat* (1861)
       Eight little tales. Cover title reads *The Happy Home and
       Other Tales.*

?1854–62   *Grand-Aunt's Pictures . . . Col TC*   H32

?1854–62   *William and Henry*   ⎫   H33
?1854–62   *Mary and her Grandmama* ⎬ No copies have been   H34
?1854–62   *John and James*   ⎭ discovered.   H35

No date.   *The Rational Exhibition.* 55 pp. Illus. *UCLA*   H36

?1854–62   *Maria and the Ladies and Other Tales.* 48 pp. Cuts. *BM*

       Five short tales, all signed by Sophia Kelly. The cover title
       is *Mrs. Sherwood's Parting Gift.* The five titles noted above
       are also likely to be the work of Mrs. Kelly.

Section ii: Chapbooks in Penny and Twopenny Series

Both sets of chapbooks are listed in the order in which they
appear on the backs of some items. Often reprinted, they came out
undated under the imprint of Darton and Clark (1836–47) and
Darton and Co. (1844–62). On the evidence of lists appearing in
other books, these dates could, in most cases, be narrowed to the
period 1840–50. The Penny Books are 7 × 11·5 cm in size; sixteen
pages long, and illustrated by a frontispiece and various little
woodcuts (which in some cases obviously inspired the story).
Eleven of the Penny Books (the exception being *Dangerous Sport*)
are reprinted in *Juvenile Tales* (Milner & Sowerby, 1861), *Univ
London Library.* The only complete set of the scarce Twopenny
Books so far identified is in the Darton Collection at Teachers'

142

College, Columbia University, N.Y. Numbers following the titles are those by which the late F. J. Harvey Darton itemized the booklets in his private catalogue, the collection not yet having been officially catalogued by its present owners. *How to Please, Willy Cary, What Could I Do Without Grandmother,* and *The Blind Gentleman* were included in *Juvenile Tales.* (K3)

Twopenny Books, like Darton's annuals, are squarish in shape and stand 14·5 cm high.

Penny Books:

Lucy's Going to School . . . Parker; Newberry	H37–48
Horses and Coaches . . . UCLA	
Land of Snow . . . Parker; UCLA	
The Useful Dog . . . UCLA	
Dangerous Sport . . . V & A	

A cautionary tale about a little boy who played with a gun, this item has a totally irrelevant frontis. displaying a fall from a rocking-horse.

Susan's First (alt. 'Feast') *Money* . . . UL; UCLA
The Flood . . . UCLA
The Honey Drop . . . UCLA
The Indian Chief . . . UCLA
The Shawl . . . UCLA
Eyes and Ears . . . UCLA
Going to the Fair . . . Parker; UCLA

(1848–62)   *My Prize Book* . . . UCLA
The twelve penny books bound together with the original illustrations and pagings.

Twopenny Books:

How to Please . . . 788. Parker; Col TC	H49–60
— Providence: [Weeden & Peek?] n.d. *AAS*	

The Parting Cup . . . 799. Col TC
Yours is the Best . . . 797. Col TC
Willy Cary (alt. Cory) . . . 793. Col TC
— Providence: [Weeden & Peek?] n.d. UCLA
Conceit Checked . . . 795. Col TC
What Could I Do Without Grandmother? . . . 786. Col TC
— Providence: Weeden & Peek [1849]
What's the Use of That? . . . 787. Col TC
Let Me Take Care of Myself . . . 791, 806. Col TC
— Providence: [Weeden & Peek?] n.d. *AAS*
The Druids of Britain . . . 798. Col TC; BM (cat. only)
The Blind Gentleman . . . 785. Col TC
The Child is but a Child . . . 790. Col TC
— Providence: Weeden & Peek. n.d. *Phil*
Comfort in Death . . . 794. Col TC; UL

J: OTHER PUBLISHERS (ORDER IS CHRONOLOGICAL ACCORDING TO FIRST WORKS PUBLISHED)
T. Hamilton, 33 Paternoster Row, and J. Taylor, 116 High Holborn.

1822–48   *The Youth's Magazine, or Evangelical Miscellany*   J1
This periodical, which had printed Jane Taylor's *Contributions of Q.Q.*, brought out tales, tracts, and articles by Mrs. Sherwood for over twenty-five years (signed at first M.M., and after 1827, M.M.S.). The earlier tales were rapidly reprinted by Houlston, Darton, Melrose, Knight and Lacey and the R.T.S., as well as by various American publishers.
After 1825, T. Hamilton published in conjunction with Adams at 33 (later 32) Paternoster Row.

1825   Preface to *Scripture Exercises*. Intended as an Introduction   J2
to Chalmers's Scripture References. Worcester: Printed by and for T. Eaton and sold by Nisbet and Westley, London; F. Houlston and Son, Wellington; and H. Mozley, Derby, pp. iii–vii (*Introduction* by Mrs. Sherwood); 90 pp. *Parker*
The *Introduction* argues for more attention to Scripture and less to the heathen classics.

1827   *Le Fevre*. A True Narrative . . . *Eng Cat*, 1801–36   J3
Reprinted by Harper in *Works*, Vol. 13 (K1)

1829   *The Millennium, or Twelve Stories* . . . [3], 164 pp. Engr. frontis.   J4
Radclyffe. *Bod*; *Osb*
   1829   *The Millennium*, etc. New York: J. Leavitt; Boston: Crocker & Brewster. 144 pp. *Am Bib* 40411; *U Kansas*

Knight and Lacey, 55 Paternoster Row.

1823–4   *The Child's Magazine* . . . 2 vols. xii, 160 pp.; xiv, 192 pp.   J5
Cuts. *Parker*; *UCLA* (Vol. I only)
Preface to Vol. I (10 numbers) explains that the magazine is a continuation of 'The Sunday School', and that the title has been altered to make it 'acceptable to children of a higher rank'. Preface to Vol. II (12 numbers) is a plea for the study of the types and emblems of Scripture.

1823   *Bible History, or Scripture its Own Interpreter* . . . xi, 204 pp.   J6
BM
According to Naomi Royde Smith's unsupported statement, this book was written by 'an anonymous male student author', and only revised by Mrs. Sherwood. It is an expression of the currently popular Millenarian theories as preached by Edward Irving and others.

1824   *The Spanish Daughter*. By the Rev. George Butt . . . Revised   —
        and corrected by his daughter, Mrs. Sherwood . . . In two
        volumes. 217; 222 pp. *BM*
        n.d. — Boston: Crocker & Brewster. Listed in *Am Cat*
        1820–52

1825   *My Uncle Timothy*, an Interesting Tale for Young Persons   J7
        . . . 91 pp. Frontis. *BM*; *U Vic, B.C.*
        Extracted from *The Youth's Magazine*, which paid £21 for
        the copyright in 1824.

1825   *Juliana Oakley*, an Autobiography (alt. a Tale) . . . 134 pp.   J8
        Engr. and 'twenty-eight embellishments'. *Osb* (2nd ed.);
        V & A (5th ed.)
        Extracted from *The Youth's Magazine* (1823), this story went
        through many printings in 1825, including one by Houlston,
        who claimed it thereafter.
        1825 — Hartford: O. D. Cooke. *Phil*

B. J. Holdsworth, 18 St. Paul's Churchyard, London.

1824   *The Bible Teacher's Manual*, Pt. III. *Evangelical Magazine*   J9
        Supplement, 1824. *NYPL*
        1827 — Pt. V, *Evangelical Magazine*, 1827

1827   *The Birthday Present*. Parker   J10

Sabbath School Union for Scotland.

1825   *Clara Stephens, or The White Rose* . . . 140 pp. *Parker*   J11
        1827   *Clara Stephens* or . . . American S.S. Union (Nos.
        330, 331 of Series XI). Frontis., Gilbert. 144 pp. *BM*

1827   *Religious Fashion, or the History of Anna*. A volume   J12
        probably first issued by the S.S.U.S., but only known
        in an edition 'revised by The Committee of Publication'
        of The American S.S.U., Philadelphia, iv, 138 pp. *BM*

Dean and Munday, Threadneedle Street, London.

1826   *The Soldier's Orphan, or The History of Maria West* . . . [3]   J13
        158 pp. Frontis. and t.-p. vignette by H. Corbould. *Bod*
        1828 — Portland: Shirley and Hyde. 143 pp. Illus. *Phil*

Longman, Rees, Orme, Brown and Green, Paternoster Row,
London

1826–7   *A Chronology of Ancient History*, illustrated by parallel   J14
        streams of time . . . 2 vols. xii, 382; iv, 524 pp. Engr.
        Frontis. S. Smith, Map. *BM*; *Boston PL*

1827 *Susannah, or The Three Guardians*   J15
     Extracted from *The Youth's Magazine*, 1825
     Revised by Sophia Kelly and reprinted, 1871
     1829 — Am. S.S.U. (No. 230, Series VII). 90 pp. *BM*;
          Phil FL

1840 *Former and Latter Rain . . . London Cat*; *Public Circular 1840*   J16
     No copy known.

1840 *A Visit to Sherwood Forest, Newstead,* etc. . . . *Eng Cat*   J17
     1835–62
     No copy known. May not be by Mrs. Sherwood.

R. B. Seeley and W. Burnside, 172 Fleet St., and L. B. Seeley and
Son, 169 Fleet St., London

1831 *Scripture Prints* [illustrating Genesis] with Explanations in   J18
     the form of Familiar Dialogue . . . viii, 254 pp. Plates (some
     signed Sears). *BM*
     1832 — New York: Pendleton and Hill. iv, 254 pp.
          Frontis., plates. *Phil FL*
     1841 *Conversations on the Bible* . . . vii, 254 pp. *BM*
          A new edition of *Scripture Prints*

1833 *The Nun* . . . 326 pp. Engr. frontis. and t.-p., S. Williams. *BM*   J19
     1834 — Princeton: Moore Baker. 326 pp. 2 plates. *NYPL*;
          Yale

1833 *The Latter Days* . . . vii, 273 pp. *BM*; *Yale*   J20

1842 *Robert and Frederick,* A Tale for Boys . . . vi, 390 pp. Engr.   J21
     S. Williams. *Osb*
     1853 — Bohn. *Harvard*; *NYPL* (1856)

1851 *Jamie Gordon, or The Orphan. Eng Cat*; *London Cat*, 1851   J22
     No copy known.

R. Wrightson (Printer), Birmingham

1828 *Theophilus,* the history of a boy deaf and dumb from birth;   J23
     written expressly for . . . the Institution for deaf and dumb
     children . . . 58 pp. *Wandsworth*

Thomas Ward (later Ward, Lock), 27 Paternoster Row, London

1835 *Sabbaths on the Continent* . . . 136 pp. *BM*   J24
     Extracted from *The Youth's Magazine*, 1832.
     Reprinted by Harper in *Works*, Vol 13 (K1)

H. K. Lewis, London

1848 *The Fairy Knoll* . . . 153 pp. *BM* (*cat. only*); *Bod* (1850)   J25
     Since H. K. Lewis was a medical publisher, it seems that
     Dr. R. J. Streeten, Mrs. Sherwood's son-in-law, may have
     used his influence as editor of the *Medical Journal.*

146

Thomas Nelson, Paternoster Row and Edinburgh

1849   *The Story Book of Wonders* . . . [5] 136 pp. 8 plates. *BM*;   J26
        Harvard
        Contents include poetry and a passage of music by others.
        Preface states that 'The design of the authoress . . . is to
        furnish a series of interesting and instructive readings for
        the young, on the Wonders of Nature. Her aim has been,
        while conveying useful information in as pleasing and
        attractive a form as possible, to lead the youthful mind to
        the great Creator of all'. The most scientific and least
        emblematic of Mrs. Sherwood's efforts to present natural
        history, it suggests that she had followed the proceedings of
        the Worcester Society for the study of science and natural
        history. Both Capt. Sherwood and Dr. Streeten were mem-
        bers. The contents of some of the papers given indicate
        that the theories expressed in *The Origin of Species* were
        known to the speakers at this time.

K: A NOTE ON COLLECTIONS OF MRS. SHERWOOD'S WORKS

The only attempt at publishing a full collected edition was made
by Harper & Bros. of New York:

1834–57   *The Works of Mrs. Sherwood*. Being the only uniform   K1
           edition ever published in the United States . . . New York,
           Harper & Bros.
           Vols. I–VIII appeared in 1834; Vols. IX–XII (*The Lady of
           the Manor*) in 1835; Vols. XIII–XIV in 1837; and Vol.
           XVI (*The History of John Marten*) in 1857.

Harper's also published a three-volume edition of *Roxobel* in
1831. Apart from this major effort, there were several minor or
partial collections published in England or the U.S.A. The chief
English firm involved was Milner & Sowerby of London (formerly
of Halifax), who took over many titles formerly published by
Darton and issued them as cheap reprints or in 'cottage library'
form.

In New York, Messrs. R. B. Carter & Bros. brought out their
'Lily Series' of Mrs. Sherwood's tales against a revival of interest
in her writing during the 1860s and 1870s. Each volume in the
series contained 108 pp. made up of one long tract tale and several
shorter ones:

1860   *Mrs. Sherwood's Popular Tales*. London: Milner & Sowerby.   K2
        ULL
        The one volume includes *The Two Knights*; *Caroline Mor-
        daunt*; *Shanty* (under the title *The Maid of Judah*); *The Idler*;
        The Cloak; *Frank and his Christmas Gift*.

1861   *Mrs. Sherwood's Juvenile Tales*. Milner & Sowerby. *ULL*   K3
        A companion to the above including all the penny books,
        several of the twopenny books, *Social Tales* and *The Brothers*
        (i.e. *Brotherly Love*).

1869 'The Lily Series', 6 volumes. New York: R. B. Carter & K4
Bros. *BM* (1871)
Vol. I *The Flowers of the Forest*; Vol. II *The Young Forester*;
Vol. III *The Little Woodman and his Dog*; Vol. IV *The Little
Beggars*; Vol. V *The Two Orphans, or the Roman Baths*; Vol. VI
Joan the Trustworthy.

1880 *The Juvenile Library*. By Mrs. Sherwood. Containing a K5
selection from her popular stories for young people. With
entirely new illustrations by Mary Sibree. London: Swan,
Sonnenschein & Co. 3 vols. *BM*

PART II
Sources Consulted

Section 1: The Evangelicals and the Evangelical Movement

Abbey, C. J. and J. H. Overton. *The English Church in the Eighteenth
Century*, Vol. II. London, 1878
Altick, R. D. *The English Common Reader* . . . Chicago, 1957
Brown, F. K. *Fathers of the Victorians* . . . Cambridge, 1961
—— *The Church in the Army*. A new edition. London, *c.* 1840
Dimond, S. G. *The Psychology of the Methodist Revival*. London, 1926
Forster, E. M. *Marianne Thornton*. A domestic biography. London, 1956
Gill, F. C. *The Romantic Movement and Methodism*. London, 1937
Hopkins, M. A. *Hannah More and her Circle*. New York, 1947
Howse, E. M. *Saints in Politics* . . . Toronto, 1952
Jones, W. *Jubilee Memorial of the Religious Tract Society* . . . London, 1850
Laird, M. A. *Missionaries and Education in Bengal* 1793–1837. Oxford,
1972.
Martin, B. *John Newton*. A biography. London, 1950
More, H. and others. *Cheap Repository Tracts*. London, 1839–46
More, H. *Moral Sketches of Prevailing Opinions and Manners*, etc. London,
1819
Richmond, L. *Annals of the Poor*, an edition. London, 1878
Robbins, W. *The Newman Brothers* . . . London, 1966
Smith, S. *Essays* reprinted from *The Edinburgh Review*. London, n.d.
Stephen, J. *Essays in Ecclesiastical Biography*, 4th edition. London, 1860
Stock, E. *History of the Church Missionary Society*, 3 vols. London, 1899
Trimmer, S. *The Oeconomy of Charity* . . . London, 1787
Wilberforce, R. I. and S. *The Correspondence of William Wilberforce*,
London, 1840
Wilberforce, W. *A Practical View of the Prevailing Religious System* . . .
Contrasted with Real Christianity. London, 1797

Section 2: Children's Books and Education in the Early Nineteenth
Century

Andreae, G. *The Dawn of Juvenile Literature in England*. Amsterdam, 1925
Bacon, G. B. 'The Literature of our Sunday Schools' in *Hours at Home*,
Vol. 10. New York, Feb.–April, 1870
Barry, F. *A Century of Children's Books*. London, 1922

Cruse, A. *The Englishman and his Books in the early Nineteenth Century.*
London, 1930
—— *The Victorians and their Books.* London, 1935
Darton, F. J. H. *Children's Books in England* . . . 2nd edition. Cambridge,
1958
—— 'Children's Books' in *Cambridge History of English Literature*, Vol.
XI, 1953
Field, Mrs. E. M. *The Child and his Book* . . . London, 1891
Grey, J. E. Introduction to *The Governess* by Sarah Fielding. London,
1968 (The Juvenile Library)
Halsey, R. V. *Forgotten Books of the American Nursery.* Boston, 1911
Kiefer, M. *American Children through their Books.* Philadelphia, 1948
Lochhead, M. *Their First Ten Years*, Victorian Childhood. London,
1956
Moses, M. *Children's Books and Reading.* New York, 1907
Neuburg, V. *The Penny Histories.* London, 1968 (The Juvenile Library)
Partridge, C. 'Evangelical Children's Books' in *Notes and Queries*, Vol.
195, Feb. 1950
Sangster, P. *Pity my Simplicity.* London, 1963
Thwaite, M. F. *From Primer to Pleasure.* London, 1963
Trimmer, S. *The Guardian of Education.* A Periodical Work . . . London,
1802–6.
Welsh, C. 'The Early History of Children's Books in New England' in
The New England Magazine . . . Vol. 26. Boston, 1899
Yonge, C. 'Didactic Fiction' in *Macmillan's Magazine* Vol. XX, Aug.
1869.

Section 3: Bibliographies, Encyclopaedias, etc.

Allibone's Dictionary of Authors, Vol. 2. 1870 ed.
The American Catalogue. New York, 1941
Block, A. *The English Novel 1740–1850.* A Catalogue . . . London, 1961
A Catalogue of the Spencer Collection . . . Preston, 1967
Catalogues of the American Sunday School Union issued between 1828–52
Chambers's Encyclopaedia, Vol. IX, 1892 ed.
Gumuchian et Cie. *Les Livres de l'Enfance du Xve au XIXe Siècle*, 2 vols.
Paris, 1930
Haviland, V. *Children's Literature.* A Guide to Reference Sources.
Washington, 1966
James, P. *Children's Books of Yesterday.* London, 1933
Muir, P. *English Children's Books 1600–1900.* London, 1954
The New Cambridge Bibliography of English Literature, Vol. III, 1969
The Osborne Collection of Early Children's Books 1566–1910. A Catalogue.
Toronto, 1958
Roscoe, S. *Newbery–Carnan–Power.* A provisional Check-list. London,
1966
Sadleir, M. *XIX Century Fiction* . . . 2 vols. London, 1951
Shaw, R. R. and R. H. Shoemaker. *American Bibliography.* A preliminary
Check-list. New York, 1958–63
Welch, d'A. 'A Bibliography of American Children's Books Printed
prior to 1821' in *Proceedings of the American Antiquarian Society*,
1963–7

Section 4: The Life and Works of Mrs. Sherwood

(a) *Life*

Cameron, G. *The Life of Mrs. Cameron*. London, 1862
Darton, F. J. H., ed. *Life and Times of Mrs. Sherwood*. London, 1910
Kelly, S., ed. *Life of Mrs. Sherwood* (chiefly autobiographical). . . .
    London, 1854
Macnaghten, A. I. J. *Daniel Corrie, his Family and Friends*. London,
    1969
Smith, N. R. *The State of Mind of Mrs. Sherwood*. London, 1946
Wilson, M. *Jane Austen and Some Contemporaries*. London, 1938

(b) *Works: Comment and Criticism*

Christian Observer and Advocate . . . May 1837, pp. 306–7
Evangelical Magazine, Vols. xxiii, xxvi, xxviii, xxix and the New Series,
    Vols. for 1823, 1824, 1827, 1829, 1831, etc.
The Living Age. Reviews of *The Life of Mrs. Sherwood* in Vol. 41 (1854),
    pp. 602–5, and Vol. 43, pp. 339–62
Keith, S. 'Gruesome Examples for Children' in *Notes and Queries*,
    Vol. 210, May 1965
Quarterly Review, 1843, pp. 25–53 (Article II 'Evangelical Novels')
Salopian Magazine and Monthly Observer, Vol. I (1815), 31 Jan., 31 Aug.,
    31 Oct., and 30 Nov. (Reviews of *Little Henry, Lucy Clare, Sergeant
    Dale*, etc.)
Times Literary Supplement, 8 Nov. 1934 (Bibliographical Notes);
    18 Jan. 1947 (Review of Smith, *State of Mind* . . .); 15 June 1951
    ('What made the Burnt Child dread the Fire?')
Worcester Miscellany, 1831 (Review of *Emancipation*), pp. 155–7

Name and Subject Index

Title Index

to works by Mrs. Sherwood (and some by Mrs. Streeten) in the Bibliography. Titles of English and American editions have been listed but there is no separate entry for sub-titles. The initial lettered reference is to the Bibliography, subsequent numbered references are to pages of the Introduction, Appendices, etc.